Lose the Lecture

Engaging Approaches to Early Childhood Professional Learning

by Teresa A. Byington, PhD

Gryphon House

Gryphon House, Inc.

www.gryphonhouse.com

Published by Gryphon House, Inc.

P. O. Box 10, Lewisville, NC 27023

800.638.0928; 877.638.7576 [fax]

Visit us on the web at www.gryphonhouse.com.

Library of Congress Cataloging-in-Publication Data

Names: Byington, Teresa A., author.

Title: Lose the lecture : engaging approaches to early childhood professional
    learning / by Teresa A. Byington.

Description: Lewisville, NC : Gryphon House, Inc., [2019] | Includes
    bibliographical references and index.

Identifiers: LCCN 2019011449 | ISBN 9780876598177 (pbk.)

Subjects: LCSH: Early childhood teachers--Training of. | Early childhood
    teachers--In-service training.

Classification: LCC LB1139.23 .B95 2019 | DDC 372.21--dc23

LC record available at https://lccn.loc.gov/2019011449

Bulk Purchase

Gryphon House books are available for special premiums and sales promotions as well as for fund-raising use. Special editions or book excerpts also can be created to specifications. For details, call 800.638.0928.

Disclaimer

Gryphon House, Inc., cannot be held responsible for damage, mishap, or injury incurred during the use of or because of activities in this book. Appropriate and reasonable caution and adult supervision of children involved in activities and corresponding to the age and capability of each child involved are recommended at all times. Do not leave children unattended at any time. Observe safety and caution at all times.

To all the amazing early childhood trainers, coaches, and professionals I have interacted with during the past twenty years!

CONTENTS

Professional Learning Communities (PLCs) and Communities of Practice (CoPs)

Mentoring and Coaching

Facilitating Effective Training Sessions

APPENDICES

PREFACE

For over ten years, I have been privileged to provide professional-learning opportunities for early childhood professionals. I love seeing adult learners make learning connections and improve their practices. One of those learners, a child-care-center director whom I'll call Tricia, shared an experience that illustrates why this work is so meaningful to me.

One day, Tricia was meeting with one of her teachers to discuss the teacher's Child Development Associate (CDA) portfolio. To see the portfolio better, Tricia moved from behind her desk and sat next to the teacher. As they talked, Tricia remembered a story (adapted from the book *Drive: The Surprising Truth about What Motivates Us* by Daniel Pink) she had heard during a professional learning session:

A new manager, Sofia (not her real name), told her staff that she had an open-door policy. When staff came to meet with Sofia in her office, she sat behind her desk and staff sat in front of it. During these meetings, Sofia's computer, emails, and phone calls frequently distracted her. At her six-month appraisal, much to her surprise, Sofia's staff rated her poorly on her communication skills. After some reflection, she realized that she was often preoccupied and dismissive when her staff tried to communicate with her.

Sofia made one simple change: she added a small table and chairs to her office. Now when staff wanted to meet with her, she left her desk and sat at the table with them, giving them her full attention. At her year-end appraisal, Sofia's staff rated her highly on her communication skills.

Recalling this story caused Tricia to notice a difference between how it felt when she sat behind her desk versus beside the teacher. Tricia recognized that she needed to change and obtained permission to add a small table and chairs to her office for meeting with staff. Six months later, Tricia found that this simple change had made a distinct difference in her relationships with her staff. She felt more connected with them, and they commented that they felt heard and understood.

As a facilitator of professional learning, I find great fulfillment in hearing how Tricia and other participants use concepts from professional-learning experiences to improve their everyday practices. Professional learning affects not only how early childhood professionals interact with each other but also how they teach and interact with children. By providing meaningful professional-learning experiences to early childhood professionals, we improve outcomes for the children and families we serve. Join me on this journey as we explore ways to incorporate rich professional learning into your program and community.

ACKNOWLEDGMENTS

Many people deserve gratitude for helping me along my journey of writing this book. I especially want to thank my husband, Brad, for his support, encouragement, and proofreading skills! Thank you to my daughter, Jenny, and son, Scott, for their love and support. Thank you to my good friend Judy Winn for giving feedback on the book. A great big thank-you to the wonderful team of trainers and coaches who shared their expertise and feedback with me: Mercedes Hutchins, Janelle Jamero, Cathy Peshlakai, Erin Skaggs, Theresa Vadala, Yohana Vasquez-Montenegro, Rebecca Vizina, and Sarah Wright. Together, we have had some amazing experiences! A big thank-you to the editorial team at Gryphon House, especially Candice Bellows and Stephanie Roselli. Sincere thanks to all the dedicated leaders, coaches, trainers, and teachers in the early childhood field who have attended my professional-learning sessions and enriched my life. And finally, thank you to all the people who have mentored, coached, and taught me throughout the years!

INTRODUCTION
Shifting from Traditional Professional Development to Engaged Professional Learning

Tanisha, a preschool teacher, has just come from a professional-development (PD) session that had no relevance to her. All teachers from her child-care center were required to attend, even though the topic turned out to be health and safety in infant-toddler classrooms. The presenter spent two hours lecturing nonstop, never even opening the floor for questions, as the teachers tried to stay awake. Tanisha leaves with no new information to help her with her most burning concern: her preschoolers' social-emotional development.

Before Tanisha reaches her car, her director, Da-eun, catches up with her. Da-eun comments that the PD session was not helpful for preschool teachers and invites Tanisha to participate in a professional-learning (PL) opportunity. Participants will learn to enhance children's social-emotional development by attending monthly training sessions, meeting with peers in a professional learning community (PLC) twice a month, and receiving weekly coaching. Tanisha likes the idea but hesitates at the time commitment and participation requirements—especially if this program turns out anything like the PD session she just came from. With cautious optimism, though, she accepts the invitation.

During the training sessions, Tanisha learns new skills for promoting social-emotional development. At the PLC meetings, she excitedly shares her successes with other preschool teachers and asks for ideas on meeting current classroom challenges. Each week, Tanisha's coach provides one-on-one support by modeling and helping Tanisha practice new skills. Tanisha begins to see marked improvement in the social-emotional development of the children in her classroom.

BRIEF INTRODUCTION TO PROFESSIONAL DEVELOPMENT AND PROFESSIONAL LEARNING

A change is occurring in early childhood education. Whereas early childhood professionals once spent a lot of time passively participating in traditional professional-development events, they now increasingly engage in ongoing, continuous professional learning. Communities of practice (CoPs), professional learning communities (PLCs), mentoring, and coaching are supplanting lectures and other less-effective means of continuing education. This book can help you implement professional learning methods into your work. First, let's examine the differences between professional development (PD) and professional learning (PL)—and why professional learning is more effective.

PD encompasses many types of informal, typically one-time learning experiences. In contrast, PL includes multifaceted, interactive, ongoing learning experiences. Because PL uses multiple formats and makes learning continuous, it makes a distinct difference in early childhood professionals' ability to transfer learning into practice. Specifically, according to Justin Markussen-Brown and his colleagues, by undertaking several types of PL simultaneously, early childhood professionals gain greater understanding of educational best practices and become more effective at implementing these practices. Strengthening practices leads to positive outcomes for children, families, and communities.

HOW TO USE THIS BOOK

This book is designed to help you think about PL in a new light. You may already engage in some aspect of PL, such as belonging to a PLC, providing coaching, or facilitating engaging training sessions. However, PL works best when a learner engages in several types simultaneously—in fact, this practice results in greater changes than one would expect from the initial investment. It is time to lose the lecture and involve early childhood professionals in engaging approaches to continuing education.

Why are you reading this book? Ask yourself the following questions:
- Do you want to gain awareness about PL?
- Do you want to enhance your cognitive understanding of PL?
- Do you want to explore your feelings about changing PL practices?
- Do you want to apply what you learn by implementing new ideas into your next PL endeavor?

I hope that you answered yes to several of the questions, because this book can help you with all of these goals. The book provides an expanded understanding of PL, encourages you to change your attitudes where needed, and (hopefully) motivates you to act to enhance your skills and practices so that, in turn, you can strengthen the practices of other early childhood professionals.

This book covers three main types of PL:
- Professional learning communities (PLCs) and communities of practice (CoPs)
- Mentoring and coaching
- Effective training sessions

You may ask, "How will this book help me strengthen the PL that I provide?" There are multiple answers to this question:
- You will learn to create effective PLCs and CoPs.
- You will identify why multifaceted PL is worth your time and effort.
- You will learn strategies for implementing effective mentoring and coaching.

- You will explore ways to help teachers become more reflective about their practices.

- You will learn to use the Reflective Strengths-Based Coaching (RSBC) Model.

- You will find step-by-step instructions for over fifty different engagement strategies.

- You will gain a greater understanding of how to meet the needs of diverse learners.

- You will learn how to be a more effective facilitator of PL.

As you read this book, reflect on how you can improve your practices and how you can help your colleagues do the same. Engaging in PL helps you participate in the long-term process of learning and thinking in new ways. Change can be difficult, even painful, but just as a butterfly emerges from its chrysalis, the early childhood profession will emerge as a stronger and more resilient entity as you and your colleagues increasingly engage in PL. Together, we will move the early childhood profession forward to have an even greater positive impact on children, families, and communities.

PART 1

PROFESSIONAL LEARNING COMMUNITIES (PLCs) AND COMMUNITIES OF PRACTICE (CoPs)

CHAPTER 1:

Professional Development versus Professional Learning

Because licensing requirements mandate that Susanne complete twelve hours of training each year, she regularly attends two-hour training sessions. Sometimes she finds them a complete waste of time, while other times she learns possible new strategies. Even then, she rarely ends up trying the new ideas because it is easier to continue teaching as she always has.

In contrast, Karina attends both training and coaching sessions. During each training session, she creates action plans for implementing specific strategies. She also meets with her coach twice a month to discuss her progress on her action plans. The coach challenges Karina to take risks and try different strategies. Change is hard, but as Karina has worked on her goals, her students have become more engaged.

PROFESSIONAL DEVELOPMENT VERSUS PROFESSIONAL LEARNING

Most professions require employees to undertake some type of continuous learning, an enterprise referred to as *professional development* (PD). Ideally, it should address current employment needs and practices. Many early childhood professionals know that PD is important, but if they associate the term with hours of excruciatingly dull lectures that have little or nothing to do with their needs or interests, it has a negative connotation. As a leader in early childhood education, you can change that perception by implementing effective *professional learning* (PL) in your organization. To bring about that change, we need to start by thoroughly examining what PD and PL are and how they differ.

In the field of education, PD focuses on helping learners gain new information and update their content knowledge. It has traditionally focused on one-time "sit-and-get" workshops, seminars, and conferences, though it also can involve more-engaging methods. In the past, PD instructors were seen as all-knowing experts, and learners were expected to passively receive whatever information their instructors presented. More recently, PD providers have begun acknowledging that every learner brings expertise to the learning experience and that adults benefit from discussing ideas. These attitudes and practices form the basis of professional learning (PL), a more-encompassing term that refers to all educational activities that prepare individuals for their professional work. Table 1.1: Comparing PD and PL outlines in more detail how PL differs from traditional PD.

Table 1.1: Comparing PD and PL

	PD	PL
FREQUENCY	One-time events	Ongoing, continuous
FORMAT	Seminars, training sessions, conferences	Coaching, PLCs, CoPs, interactive training series, virtual platforms
FOCUS	Gaining new information Updating content knowledge	Applying information Changing skills and practices
EXPERTISE	Instructor is the expert and disseminates all knowledge	Instructor and learners share expertise
PRESENTATION STYLE	Inactive Passive learning Unidirectional Direct instruction Lecture One size fits all	Active Interactive learning Multidirectional Facilitated discussions Reflective inquiry Individualized
COMPONENTS	Fixed time and space with limited inquiry and reflection Prescribed	Flexible time and space for inquiry and reflection
LEARNERS	Passive recipients of knowledge Dependent on instructor	Have self-determination and ownership of learning Autonomous
PARTICIPATION	Mandatory Participants have no voice in content	Optional Participants have a voice in content platforms
TECHNOLOGY	Limited Used to share instructor's content with participants	Generally included Used to expand learning and participation Assists in constructing knowledge
DIMENSIONS	Learners involved in only one type of PD at a time (for example, attending training sessions only)	Learners involved in multiple types of PL at a time (for example, simultaneously attending training series, receiving coaching, and participating in communities of practice)

FREQUENCY AND FORMAT

These categories are intertwined, so we will examine them together.

PD frequently takes place as a discrete event that lasts a few hours or days, such as a seminar or conference. Professionals come to the event, receive information from an "expert," and leave. Theoretically, they then go back to their programs and change their practices. However, all too often the motivation to change quickly dissipates, frequently because learners lack time or support for making changes. Other urgent matters usually take precedence. This pattern is unfortunate because a great deal of time, effort, and money go into preparing most PD events.

In contrast, PL involves an ongoing process of inquiry and reflection. It occurs over longer periods of time. Some examples include participating in a coaching partnership over a nine-month period and attending a monthly CoP for several years. Instead of attending separate, unrelated training sessions, learners attend series of training sessions on related topics and receive coaching with the same focus. Additionally, learners interact in person or virtually through professional learning communities (PLCs) or communities of practice (CoPs). Intentionally focused PL leads to greater improvement in teaching practices.

FOCUS

In both PD and PL, participants gain new information and update their content knowledge. PD's focus usually stops here, but PL emphasizes helping participants to learn, evaluate, and change skills and practices. While PD typically only provides information, PL teaches participants how to incorporate that knowledge into what they do every day. For example, a PD session might consist of a lecture on the importance of positive discipline in the classroom. A PL session on the same topic, however, would likely include discussions, case studies, and practice time to help participants learn how to effectively implement positive-guidance strategies in their own classrooms. Participants would also learn about and practice these skills during coaching and PLC or CoP sessions.

EXPERTISE

In traditional PD, the instructor is considered *the* expert. He disseminates all the information that learners "need." In PL, trainers honor learners' expertise and not only invite but expect them to share it. Learners also share expertise with peers in PLCs and CoPs. During coaching sessions, coaches encourage teachers to be reflective and find answers within themselves. Coaches also acknowledge each teacher as the expert on the children in his classroom.

PRESENTATION STYLE AND COMPONENTS

Because these categories are intertwined, we will examine them together.

In traditional PD, the presentation style is frequently passive. The instructor uses a direct-instruction, one-directional approach, such as lecture, based on a one-size-fits-all philosophy. Learners "sit and get." When supervisors mandate such prescribed PD, employees often perceive it as nonessential and irrelevant.

PL requires participants to collaborate and take greater responsibility for their own learning. The presentation style is multidirectional, as the participants and instructors learn from each other. Sessions are interactive, with learners involved in facilitated discussions and other active learning methods. These activities help learners reflectively inquire about what they currently do and what they want to do. This is especially true during one-on-one coaching sessions or small-group peer discussions in PLCs or CoPs. Because of its ongoing nature, PL provides learners with time and space to learn deeply.

LEARNERS

In traditional PD, participants are passive recipients of knowledge, primarily listening to lecture-style presentations. They depend on the instructor for their learning.

PL encourages active learning, and participants have a lot of control over the learning process. In coaching, learners give input on potential goals and then create shared goals with their coaches. Within PLCs and CoPs, participants take ownership of their learning by identifying solutions to their own problems and concerns. As learners interact, they construct their own professional knowledge and then apply it to their individual situations.

PARTICIPATION

In PD, learners generally do not have a say in what the content will be or how they will learn it. Attending the PD session may be mandatory, and the topic may or may not be applicable to a given learner's situation.

In PL, participants have a say in what and how they learn. During coaching, learners help select the specific goals they will work on. Within PLCs and CoPs, learners discuss their concerns and topics of interest.

TECHNOLOGY

Traditional PD involves limited technology use. At most, instructors may present content using programs such as PowerPoint.

In PL, technology serves as a tool to expand interactions, increase participation, and help learners construct knowledge. By using virtual platforms, blogs, online discussion groups, and shared documents, learners interact to evaluate and improve child outcomes. In fact, technology enables peers around the world to participate in the same PL opportunities. Coaches can work remotely with teachers. CoPs can meet virtually and include larger and more-diverse participants. Groups can work on shared projects and never actually meet in person. Technology is an important tool for enhancing the possibilities of PL participation.

DIMENSIONS

Traditional PD generally has a single dimension, meaning that a learner participates in one time-limited PD event. Early childhood professionals are busy, so participating in only one type of PD takes less time and effort.

In contrast, PL has multiple dimensions. A learner typically participates in two or more types of PL at any given time. For example, Laura might attend the monthly meeting of her PLC on

Monday morning, go to an interactive training session on Wednesday night, and have her weekly conversation with her mentor on Friday afternoon. Although PL takes more time and effort than traditional PD, that investment results in more meaningful changes to professional practices.

OTHER BENEFITS OF PL FOR EARLY CHILDHOOD PROFESSIONALS

As we've seen, traditional PD has limited impact. I am not advocating that all traditional PD events be eliminated—there is certainly a place for local, state, and national conferences. Instead, I want to see more opportunities for early childhood professionals to experience multifaceted PL throughout the year because PL has a higher probability of leading to lasting change. PL also provides these benefits:

- Inspires creative thought by encouraging learners to think in new ways

- Focuses on positive, strengths-based (what learners are doing well) ideas as it helps learners seek solutions. We will discuss strengths-based approaches in detail in chapter 8.

- Promotes respectful sharing by encouraging all learners to offer ideas

- Provides opportunities for learners to reflect on current and future practices

- Looks at telescopic (big-picture) and microscopic (detail-oriented) views of situations

- Encourages evidence-based teaching

- Becomes a support network for participants to share expertise and learn from each other

This last benefit is particularly important. Given the nature of their responsibilities, early childhood professionals have limited opportunities to discuss professional practices with peers during an average workday. These circumstances often produce a sense of professional isolation. But during PL, learners create networks of connections as they meet and collaborate. For instance, during one CoP that I facilitated, a participant explained that the CoP had helped to validate her challenges and concerns. She was the director of a child-care center, and by participating in the CoP, she had discovered that she and other directors all faced similar issues. This revelation reduced her sense of isolation. Another director stated that before participating in a CoP, she didn't have anyone (aside from her husband) with whom she could share her struggles. The CoP helped her engage in problem-solving discussions about professional practices in a safe environment.

CHAPTER 2:

Overview of PLCs and CoPs

Latesha is a member of a professional learning community (PLC) for preschool teachers at her school. The group meets twice a month to discuss child outcomes and identify ways to improve practices. Recently, the PLC has been examining the results from a literacy assessment. Each teacher was given the results for the children in her classroom and asked to look for areas that needed strengthening. Latesha discovered that the children in her classroom were struggling with receptive language. Using ideas and support from the PLC members, she created an action plan and has been implementing new language strategies in her classroom. She looks forward to attending the next PLC session and sharing the positive changes she has seen in the children.

WHAT ARE PLCs AND CoPs?

Two common forms of PL are professional learning communities (PLCs) and communities of practice (CoPs). Both PLCs and CoPs are groups of professionals who regularly come together to discuss ideas, gain knowledge, and improve their practices. The two groups differ, however, in their other objectives and in their membership, structure and leadership, and focus. Table 2.1: Comparing PLCs and CoPs compares these features, which are taken from the work of Selena Blankenship and Wendy Ruona, Richard DuFour and Robert Eaker, and Etienne Wenger.

Table 2.1: Comparing PLCs and CoPs

	PLCs	CoPs
OBJECTIVES	To help professionals gain knowledge and improve practices To improve child outcomes To influence program cultures	To help professionals gain knowledge and improve practices To network and collaborate on a topic of shared interest
MEMBERSHIP	Usually mandatory for those working in a specific organization Includes staff from the same school or program	Voluntary, based on interest in topic Group size varies May include members from multiple organizations
STRUCTURE AND LEADERSHIP	Formal Facilitators chosen by (or are) administrators and provide extensive structure and guidance Smaller collaborative teams may be assigned within main PLC	Often informal Have facilitators but emphasize collaboration among members, often in small peer learning teams
COMMON AREAS OF FOCUS	Common areas of focus Measurable changes (child outcomes) Shared mission, vision, and values Action Experimentation Continuous improvement Participant accountability	Improving practice Collaboration Sharing knowledge about topic or topics of interest Building relationships Joint problem solving

OBJECTIVES

In this context, objectives are the reasons why a PLC or CoP is meeting. For both group types, the objectives drive the group's work and focus.

The objectives of a PLC are to improve child outcomes and to influence program cultures. The specific objectives of a given PLC are often driven by assessment results.

The objective of a CoP is for participants to improve their skills and practices by sharing their expertise. Through these ongoing interactions, members decrease isolation, increase collaboration, and build relationships that strengthen both individuals and the group. They also share new strategies that enhance their abilities.

MEMBERSHIP

If the leadership of an organization decides to create a PLC, membership is generally mandatory for all staff. This makes sense—every staff member contributes to the culture and achievements of a program, so every staff member must be part of any attempt to change these elements.

Membership and participation in a CoP is usually voluntary and based on common interests or concerns. For example, a CoP can focus on leadership, language and literacy, or teaching infants and toddlers. These common factors make the CoP experience relevant to daily tasks and can increase buy-in from members. In many CoPs, a core group of members participates in most activities, while other members are less involved but still find value in being part of the group. CoPs may have anywhere from a few participants meeting in person to hundreds of members meeting through virtual platforms. These platforms also mean that CoPs can grow beyond organizational or geographic boundaries. Members from various organizations, cities, states, and even countries can all participate in the same CoP.

STRUCTURE AND LEADERSHIP

A PLC has formal leadership and structure. Administrators typically set up a PLC and assign a facilitator to lead it; in fact, the facilitator often is an administrator. The facilitator has primary responsibility for making sure that the PLC functions smoothly and that the members have the resources they need. A PLC frequently functions as a whole group, but members may also work in smaller collaborative teams within the PLC.

CoPs usually have informal leadership provided by either group members or administrators. When group members provide leadership, they experience the benefits of peer learning. For example, in a CoP that I facilitated, the members decided to meet at a different child-care center each month so they could tour various facilities as part of the CoP. This activity allowed the centers' directors to assume leadership and showcase for their colleagues the features and strengths of their programs.

COMMON AREAS OF FOCUS

Richard DuFour and Robert Eaker identify several areas of focus for PLCs. To ensure unified effort, members of a PLC share common goals and values. In support of those ideals, the group members focus on instructional results, or how instruction affects children's learning, and seek to improve specific child outcomes. They use collaboration, reflective dialogue, peer coaching, action plans, and feedback to explore questions and experiment with strategies. Action and results are top priorities, and group members hold each other accountable for implementing change. They respond to assessment data and determine measureable goals that foster improvement. Members strive to reach both consensus and viable solutions.

A CoP focuses on sharing knowledge, building relationships, and using joint problem solving to address the focus area. The CoP provides a place for members to share challenges, brainstorm collectively, and explore solutions. By sharing their perspectives and experiences, group members also develop new ideas and learn best practices. For example, during a CoP session on coaching that I facilitated, participants were asked to identify challenges that arise during coaching sessions. Participants formed groups to discuss shared challenges, and each group was assigned to create at least two possible solutions. The groups then shared their solutions, and the participants gained new ideas for tackling the difficulties they faced.

KEYS TO EFFECTIVE PLCs AND CoPs

Despite their differences, effective PLCs and CoPs both have certain key characteristics. These qualities take time and effort to develop. Let's briefly look at each one.

PURPOSE

A common purpose is essential to a PL group. For best results, the group members should help to determine the purpose, rather than a facilitator or administrator selecting it, and all members should commit to achieving it.

CONSISTENCY

A successful PL group allows members to meet over a sustained period of time to develop relationships. When members interact regularly, they become more comfortable working together. These consistently safe environments help members learn how to be open to new ideas and seek creative solutions. They have time to reflect on their own and others' practices. Because members are willing to learn continuously, they create group cultures that support taking risks and trying innovative approaches.

COMMUNICATION

Clear communication is critical to all types of PL. To promote this practice within your group, learn the communication behaviors of each group member. Some may be reserved; others may love to talk. Some may be flexible and accommodating; others may forcefully present strong opinions. Effective group communication takes time and effort. A strong facilitator can help to establish an open, respectful climate.

RESPECT AND TRUST

Groups that interact respectfully also develop understanding and trust. This essential practice can be tricky, especially if personalities or viewpoints clash. Try this exercise to start your group's process of building respect and trust. This activity could also be a useful exercise for the first meeting of a new PLC or CoP.

Activity: Respect-and-Trust List

Materials

1 sheet of lined paper per participant

pens or pencils

1. Prior to the meeting, copy Table 2.2: Behaviors That Erode or Build Trust onto a PowerPoint slide.

2. During the meeting, pass out a sheet of paper (and a pen or pencil, if needed) to each participant.

3. Ask participants to think about what they need to respect and trust someone. What do they expect that person to do and say? What behaviors might cause them to mistrust the person instead? Invite participants to write down their ideas and discuss them in small groups.

4. Display the slide with Table 2.2, and have participants compare their answers to the ones in the table (which were created by a group of early childhood professionals who also performed this activity).

5. Lead a whole-group discussion on what the participants found. Ask, "Do any of these behaviors surprise you? What other ideas could you add to your list?"

Table 2.2: Behaviors That Erode or Build Trust

Erode	Build
• Disregarding others' feelings	• Keeping commitments
• Gossiping	• Validating others' feelings
• Favoritism	• Open communication, respect
• Negativity	• Accountability
• False pretenses	• Active listening
• Self-centeredness	• Keeping your word
• Blaming	• Empathy
• Dishonesty	• Problem solving
• Inconsistency	• Honesty
• Self-serving behaviors	• Integrity
	• Taking responsibility

STRATEGIES FOR STRENGTHENING PLCs AND CoPs

Any important endeavor will face challenges, and PLCs and CoPs are no exception. Effective groups are flexible and persistent in solving problems. To strengthen PLCs and CoPs and build their resilience, try these strategies.

SELECT SKILLED FACILITATORS

Facilitators have two main responsibilities. First, they take charge of (or assign other group members to handle) most of the group's administrative duties, such as arranging logistics (securing a meeting space, arranging furniture, and setting up technology) and communicating pertinent information to group members. Second, and more importantly, facilitators guide the flow of each session and ensure that all voices are heard within the group. They ask meaningful questions, invite members to share ideas, and help members reflect on both sides of issues. They minimize distractions and difficult behaviors, adapt to changing situations, and promote a common vision.

Case Study: An (In)effective Facilitator

Rutna has been asked to facilitate a PLC. She has never been a facilitator before, but she is ready for the first session. When the PLC members arrive, Rutna hands out a set agenda with specific time frames for each item. She tightly controls the discussion, doing most of the talking, cutting members off if they go over the allotted time for a topic, and dismissing ideas that differ from hers.

At the end of the session, Rutna is pleased with her performance; however, she later learns that many people left frustrated. After some reflection, Rutna decides to research more about being an effective facilitator. Based on her findings, she commits to changing her practices.

At the next PLC session, Rutna presents a flexible agenda with no defined time frames and asks members to help decide which topics to discuss. She then asks the members to create guidelines for group interactions. During the discussion, Rutna follows protocols to ensure that everyone can share ideas. She speaks much less than she did during the first session, asks guiding questions, and listens to all responses. The group has a meaningful discussion, and at the end, several members thank Rutna for facilitating.

This story demonstrates some of the differences between effective and ineffective facilitators. Here are some additional characteristics and behaviors of effective facilitators:

• Sensitive to group members' emotional and intellectual states

• Culturally responsive

• Welcome diverse perspectives

• Value and advocate for each member's contributions

• Think quickly and anticipate potential conflicts

• Listen to learn about the thoughts and perspectives of members

• Ask probing questions to determine underlying issues

Facilitators have particularly important roles in PLCs, so chapter 3 discusses those responsibilities in detail.

USE PROTOCOLS

Protocols are guidelines that provide structure to group conversations. For example, a protocol might require that participants only provide positive solutions to an issue rather than air complaints and criticisms. A different protocol could direct participants to keep the conversation objective by sharing concrete evidence instead of opinions, conjecture, or speculation.

Most groups need multiple protocols to ensure orderly, productive discussions. Ideally, group members develop protocols together. Thereafter, the facilitator ensures that everyone follows the protocols during group meetings.

Try using this sample protocol to promote meaningful discussions among smaller segments of the main group. This protocol ensures that everyone has a chance to speak fully and that quick thinkers or responders do not dominate conversations.

Sample Protocol: Triad Protocol

1. Have participants split into groups of three (triads). Instruct the members of each triad to designate one person as Person 1, one person as Person 2, and one person as Person 3.

2. Ask the triads to think about a specific question, such as, "How can you build strong relationships with culturally diverse families?"

3. Explain that within the triads, each person will give her answer without any interruptions. Person 1 will speak first, then Person 2, and then Person 3. The other triad members can make comments and ask questions only after all three people have spoken without interruption.

4. When everyone finishes commenting, pose another question. This time, explain that Person 2 will go first, then Person 3, and then Person 1. Again, each person will speak uninterrupted, and then other group members can make comments and ask questions after everyone has shared.

5. For each question, have the triad members rotate their speaking order.

CREATE CLIMATE-OF-CARE GUIDELINES

In a PL group, members want to find acceptance, respect, and supportive relationships within an emotionally safe environment. *Climate-of-care guidelines* are general behavior expectations for the group. They differ from protocols, which structure group conversations. Climate-of-care guidelines prove especially useful when personal problems or negative experiences taint how a person interacts with others. Following climate-of-care guidelines creates an environment where members feel safe to share.

To establish climate-of-care guidelines, follow these steps:

1. Ask each group member to reflect on the best and worst group conversations in which she has participated and to identify the types of behaviors that accompanied each conversation.

2. Have participants each write down several answers to this question: "What behaviors do you think promote positive group conversations?"

3. Split the participants into groups of four or five. Instruct each group to select a note taker, discuss the question, and formulate potential climate-of-care guidelines, answering these questions for each guideline: "What does the guideline *look* like? What does it *sound* like? What does it *feel* like?"

4. Invite each small group to share several guidelines with the large group. Direct the large group to look for commonalities in the ideas shared.

5. Lead the large group in cooperatively determining what guidelines everyone will follow during interactions. Write down these guidelines and create a chart (you might have to finish it after the session).

6. At the beginning of each subsequent session, post the chart where everyone can see it, and review the guidelines with the entire group.

Having worked in PL for years, I have watched many groups conduct this exercise. Here are some of the climate-of-care guidelines they have created:

- Communicate respectfully.

- Be attentive listeners.

- Share the floor.

- Support and encourage each other.

- Infuse interactions with joy.

- Stay on task.

- Keep confidences.

These sample guidelines demonstrate some of the core values in a climate of care. Group members demonstrate respect by listening to different perspectives, staying on topic, and avoiding distracting activities, such as texting and side conversations. As members truly listen to each other and are open to diverse ideas, they benefit from others' experiences. Relationships grow stronger as group members validate each other's thoughts and respond with support and encouragement.

Groups should revisit their climate-of-care guidelines at the beginning of each session. The process can be as simple as having a group member say something like this: "We agreed on these things: We listen to all voices. We support and encourage each other and seek to understand each person's perspective. We respectfully provide constructive feedback. Our goal is to enhance our teaching practices and improve child outcomes." For variety, and to reinforce the message for each person, a different group member could review the guidelines at each meeting.

CULTIVATE DEEP LISTENING

PL group conversations allow members to connect with and learn about each other by listening to different perspectives. But just listening is insufficient. Deep listening guides group members to discover what they care about and leads to more-meaningful interactions.

Deep listening involves more than just paying attention or receiving knowledge. It even moves beyond assimilating ideas. It is hearing the deeper meaning behind the words, connecting to the speaker, reflecting on the message, and embracing it without feeling the need to immediately respond. Someone at a conference I attended said that deep listening is two hearts communicating. I really like that sentiment.

To be a deep listener, a person must be present. She must silence her mind and receive the message as a gift freely given. She gives thanks for that gift by taking time to understand and appreciate the message. This practice gives the speaker the sense that she matters and is understood.

As new ideas sometimes create dissonance, a deep listener also learns to be comfortable with being uncomfortable. This capacity is crucial because a transformative process of growth takes place during times of discomfort and self-reflection. In her book *Turning to One Another*, Margaret Wheatley says, "There is no power for change greater than a community discovering what it cares about." As your group discovers what it cares about, the members become more willing and able to change. Wheatley also reminds people to consider what's possible instead of what's wrong.

EXPLORE DIFFERENT PERSPECTIVES

As PL groups explore topics of interest, disagreements often arise among group members. Try this activity to practice respectfully expressing and listening to diverse viewpoints.

Activity: The Un-Debate

1. Before the group meeting, select a topic or question about which group members have a variety of opinions. (Some ideas appear at the end of this activity.)

2. Explain that the goal of the Un-Debate is to learn to value and understand other perspectives on the chosen topic. Each participant will have one minute to share her point of view and her reasoning. During that time, everyone else will silently listen. When she finishes, the rest of the group will validate her ideas by saying, "Thank you for sharing."

3. Choose a person to go first. Make sure that the other participants listen silently until she finishes, and then lead the group in saying, "Thank you for sharing."

4. Repeat this process until everyone has shared her thoughts.

5. After the last person speaks, invite participants to comment on and ask clarifying questions about what others have said, provided this dialogue is supportive and nonjudgmental.

Here are some potential topics for this exercise:

• What mealtime practices do you think child-care centers should have?

• What is your personal philosophy about messy play versus keeping clothes clean?

• How do you think children should address teachers and other adults in early childhood classrooms?

• What do you think are appropriate guidance techniques for toddlers?

• What types of behaviors do you think demonstrate trust and respect within a work environment?

When individuals genuinely listen to others' points of view, their own minds become more open. PL-group participants often state, "I never thought about it that way," or, "That's an interesting idea." These explorations build trust within the group and help members learn to value, even embrace, new ways of thinking.

ADDRESS DIFFICULT BEHAVIORS

One of the facilitator's major responsibilities is handling challenging behaviors from group members. Some members may be inattentive, disruptive, or disrespectful or may act in ways that disrupt the learning environment. However, the facilitator must not join or promote arguments. She needs to foster dialogue that focuses on creating understanding. Members may need to agree to disagree.

Try these ideas to address difficult behaviors:

• Redirect the behavior by using lighthearted humor. For instance, if you notice Koji looking at his phone instead of participating, try saying in a joking tone, "Koji, come back! We need you!"

• Remind group members of protocols and guidelines, particularly ones that promote respect, participation, and positivity. Follow these directives yourself.

• Be sensitive and acknowledge differences.

• Strive to achieve consensus.

• Seek to understand the emotions behind words.

• Remain impartial and open-minded during group interactions.

• Make the PLC a safe, neutral zone where divergent ideas are discussed respectfully.

• Foster open, productive dialogue.

• Ask members to focus on the group's purpose instead of on their personal agendas.

• Request help from other group members.

• Speak to disruptive individuals privately about specific concerns.

For more information about dealing with challenging behaviors in adult learners, see chapter 13.

ONGOING EVALUATION

The facilitator should periodically assess what is going well in her PLC or CoP and what could be improved. Participants' priorities and goals change over time, so the facilitator needs to ensure that the group focus stays relevant to its members.

Facilitators can use many evaluations to check the performance of PL groups. Cynthia Blitz and Rebecca Schulman have compiled a list of forty-nine of these instruments, which you may wish to consult. Table 3.1: Types of Evaluations compares five common evaluations: formative, process, outcome, SWOT (strengths, weaknesses, opportunities, and threats), and summative. These types of evaluations can be used throughout the life cycle of a PLC or CoP. Both group types go through four distinct phases:

1. *Development phase:* Potential members are identified and invited to participate, and the organization and logistics of the group are developed.

2. *Early-implementation phase:* Members come together to learn about the group's objectives and desired outcomes and to develop working relationships. This is a good time for making adjustments to match participants' specific needs.

3. *Program-delivery phase:* The group is up and functioning on a regular basis. This phase can last for months or years.

4. *Program-completion phase:* The program is ending. This phase includes any follow-up activities with participants.

Table 3.1: Types of Evaluations

	What It Measures	**When to Use It**
FORMATIVE	Program development Program improvement	Development phase Early-implementation phase
PROCESS	Program implementation Program structures and supports	Program-delivery phase
OUTCOME	Changes in members' knowledge, skills, and practices	Periodically throughout program
SWOT (STRENGTHS, WEAKNESSES, OPPORTUNITIES, AND THREATS)	Internal factors (strengths and weaknesses) External factors (opportunities and threats)	Periodically (for example, yearly) throughout program-delivery phase
SUMMATIVE	Program effectiveness	Periodically (for example, yearly) throughout program-delivery phase Program-completion phase

Formative Evaluation

A *formative evaluation* assesses and helps improve a PL group early in its existence. In the development phase, this might involve asking members to identify their priorities and interests prior to the first meeting. In the early-implementation phase, a formative evaluation might ask group members what is working well and what needs improvement to enhance the group experience.

Process Evaluation

A *process evaluation* examines whether the PL group is operating as it was intended to. This type of evaluation looks at the processes of implementation, the group's structures, and the types of services offered in the group. A process evaluation could ask group members to rate how well the group is being facilitated and whether the members are receiving adequate communication and supports.

Outcome Evaluation

An *outcome evaluation* examines the effectiveness of a PL group in producing change or generating positive outcomes. For example, because PLCs are often focused on improving specific child outcomes, an outcome evaluation for a PLC would examine whether the group members have achieved the desired child outcomes.

SWOT Analysis

Periodic SWOT analysis helps to identify internal and external PL-group factors. The internal factors are the group's strengths and weaknesses. Strengths could include participants' capabilities and knowledge and the resources available to the group. The weaknesses are areas in which the group needs improvement, such as enhancing communication between sessions. The external factors are opportunities for and threats to the group, including outside factors that influence it. For example, a CoP might have an opportunity to collaborate with a potential funding source. A threat to a PLC might be economic factors within the community that are causing high rates of staff turnover.

Summative Evaluation

A *summative evaluation* takes place at the end of a PL group to determine its effectiveness. Alternatively, a summative evaluation could take place on a yearly or other regular basis to identify specific changes within that time period. For example, a summative evaluation could determine whether participating in a CoP led teachers to make specific changes in their practices.

SHOULD I CREATE A PLC OR A CoP?

You should create a PLC if these factors apply to your situation:

- The group members will all come from the same organization.

- You want to focus on obtaining specific, measurable results (such as increasing the number of words children use in participants' classrooms).

- You want to build capacity for implementing change in your organization's culture.

- You want to focus on what children are doing and achieving.

- You are interested in systematically improving children's learning.

- You are more concerned about the results of your actions than the process.

- You are interested in achieving common goals and responding to data.

You should create a CoP if these factors apply to your situation:

- The group members will include participants from different organizations.

- You want to focus on a shared concern or topic of interest.

- You want group members to have opportunities to deepen their knowledge and expertise through interactions.

- You are more concerned about the process than the results.

- You want to focus on collaboration and joint problem solving.

CHAPTER 3:

Professional Learning Communities in Early Childhood Education

Francesca was recently hired to oversee a group of fifteen early childhood coaches. Although she witnesses some positive coaching conversations, Francesca also notices several coaches using a deficit-based approach, focusing on what teachers are doing wrong in their classrooms. She is concerned about the overall coaching culture in her group.

With her supervisor's approval, Francesca establishes a PLC for the coaches that focuses on strengths-based coaching. At the first session, the group creates this purpose statement: "We inspire teachers to make improvements in their classrooms so that children achieve optimum development." Focusing on this purpose, the coaches begin addressing common concerns and learning from each other about strengths-based coaching strategies. It takes time, but Francesca is pleased to see the coaches connecting with each other and the coaching culture slowly beginning to shift.

SETTING UP A PLC

As a leader in your organization, you will likely serve as the driving force behind a PLC and become its facilitator. So what exactly do you do to set up a PLC? There are three main steps: determine your *why*, choose a focus, and determine the structure of your sessions.

DETERMINE YOUR WHY

To become and stay involved in a PLC, early childhood professionals need to feel that the experience benefits them. They need to know why the PLC (or any kind of PL) is worth their time and efforts—that is, beyond simply meeting job requirements to retain employment. Thus, for a PLC to succeed, you need to determine its *why*. In his TED Talk "How Great Leaders Inspire Action," Simon Sinek asks, "What's your purpose? What's your cause? What's your belief? And why should anyone care?" He further states, "It's those who start with 'why' that have the ability to inspire those around them." In this context, the *why* is a specific question or challenge that demonstrates the need for PL.

For many PLCs, the *why* is a shared belief among the group members. The following list gives some examples:

- **Child-care-center staff:** "We believe in providing high-quality, inclusive care so that all children and families thrive within our diverse community of learners."

- **Early childhood trainers:** "We believe in facilitating engaging learning opportunities that give teachers the knowledge and skills to improve their teaching practices."

For one PLC of pre-K teachers, the *why* emerged from participating in a quality initiative. Classrooms in their program (which I will call Learning Tree Preschool) had been evaluated using the Early Childhood Environment Rating Scale-Revised (ECERS-R) and the Classroom Assessment Scoring System (CLASS). The results indicated that the teachers could strengthen children's interactions and experiences in learning centers. For the Learning Tree teachers, the why was as follows: "We believe in enhancing children's experiences within learning centers so that they achieve optimum cognitive and social-emotional development."

CHOOSE A FOCUS

Once you have your *why*, you can choose the focus of your PLC: what you will do within the group to meet your purpose. Let's continue our examples from the previous section:

- **Child-care center staff:** "We focus on ways to promote inclusive practices within diverse communities."

- **Early childhood trainers:** "We focus on creating engaging learning environments and experiences for adult learners."

- **Learning Tree teachers:** "We focus on creating experiences in learning centers that promote children's cognitive and social-emotional development."

To identify a focus for your PLC, try these methods:

- Ask potential members to complete a survey or a needs assessment to identify specific interests and needs.

- Hold group discussions to determine topics of interest.

- With key stakeholders, discuss concerns and emerging issues.

DETERMINE THE STRUCTURE OF YOUR SESSIONS

Once you have a why (the shared purpose) and a focus (how the group will address that purpose), you need to decide how your PLC sessions will work. How often will you meet? How long will sessions be? What will happen at the session? Will you bring in guest speakers? have reading assignments? discuss questions? Because you will likely serve as the facilitator, you may be tempted to simply make executive decisions for all these matters. However, you will have greater buy-in from participants if you involve them in these choices.

Once the Learning Tree teachers knew their why and their focus, they collaborated to determine how their PLC sessions would function. As a result, they dedicated one day per month for PL. PL days included training and PLC sessions, both centered on a specific topic (such as promoting cognitive development in science and math centers). During the training sessions, the teachers learned ways to improve learning-center experiences through specific teaching practices.

During the PLC sessions, the teachers split into small groups, each of which selected a facilitator. (Notice that the facilitator role is so important in a PLC that even small groups have facilitators.) The small-group facilitators asked each group member to share one idea that had stuck out to him from the day's training session. After everyone had shared, the small-group facilitators invited their group members to ask questions and comment about what they had heard.

Next, based on the day's topic, the small-group facilitators invited their group members to read certain sections from the book *All about the ECERS-R* by Debby Cryer, Thelma Harms, and Cathy Riley. Once finished, group members reviewed and reflected on the related ECERS-R assessment data from their individual classrooms and pondered their desired outcomes. Then they responded to guided handouts with prompts similar to these:

- Describe your current practices related to [the day's topic].

- What is working well in your classroom?

- What opportunities for growth do you have in this area?

- What new practices would you like to implement in your classroom?

- What ideas would you like to gain from other group members?

After completing their handouts, group members shared highlights from their reflections and discussed ideas for enhancing their practices. From these discussions, teaching teams created plans of action for meeting their goals and identified any additional resources they would need. Members then shared their plans and discussed how to hold each other accountable for carrying them out. For instance, members of some teaching teams contacted each other weekly to discuss progress.

During subsequent PLC sessions, participants reported to small groups of peers about what they had done in their classrooms. Group members brought in examples of children's work and discussed how to further enhance learning experiences. If someone had encountered issues when implementing new practices, the small groups would troubleshoot and share additional strategies. Sometimes group members committed to do additional research related to the day's topic and to report at the next session. (Appendix A contains examples of discussion topics and guiding questions from this PLC.)

Accountability is a critical component of PLCs. Being accountable not only pushes PLC members to act on their learning but also helps them share the results of that learning and celebrate the effects their efforts have on children, families, and communities. Members of PLCs can informally hold each other accountable by setting up periodic check-ins, reporting on their progress toward goals at each session, and sharing concrete examples of what they have accomplished (such as photos or videos from their classrooms—after obtaining the necessary permissions, of course). Participants can formally hold each other accountable by reporting the results of classroom and child assessment data in PLC sessions. To show accountability to families and community members, PLC members might compile photos and stories demonstrating what the members have learned in the PLC, how they have implemented that learning in their classrooms, and what effects it has had on children.

RESPONSIBILITIES OF THE FACILITATOR

As an administrator, you will likely serve as the facilitator for any PLC formed in your organization. A strong facilitator is essential for a successful PLC. Facilitators keep the group organized and focused (both during and between meetings), empower the group, and hold members accountable for their actions. When members work in small groups during PLC meetings, each group chooses a temporary facilitator to handle these duties.

MAINTAINING COMMUNICATION

The facilitator takes the lead in determining the best ways to meet and communicate, whether in person or virtually. He maintains communication with all group members, keeps everyone's contact information up to date, and orients new members on group norms and practices. He helps members come together to make decisions and reach consensus. He also conducts ongoing assessments to identify group priorities and evaluate whether the PLC is meeting its objectives.

KEEPING THE GROUP ON TASK

One of a facilitator's main challenges is to keep the group focused. Though this task can be challenging at times, a few strategies can help him prevent and recover from conversational detours.

Prior to a PLC session, the facilitator can create a "parking lot," such as a shared file (for virtual meetings) or a piece of flip-chart paper (for in-person meetings), where members can write down or post any off-topic ideas. These notes then provide prompts for later discussions. This practice reassures group members that their thoughts will not be overlooked or forgotten, even if they do not relate to the current topic of discussion. In turn, this reassurance enables everyone to focus on the current conversation.

At the beginning of a session, the facilitator should state the objectives and guiding questions of the day to remind the participants of what they want to accomplish and discuss. If the conversation later veers off course, the facilitator can refocus it by restating the designated topic. For example, he might say, "Remember, we're talking about strategies for modeling language right now." He can also use humor to redirect the discussion, such as by saying in a joking tone, "Oh no, we're getting off topic. Quick, come back!"

CULTIVATING STRONG GROUP ENGAGEMENT

The facilitator cultivates strong group engagement by helping members connect outside of the PLC. Between sessions, he distributes information related to the meetings. Some facilitators set up a blog, wiki, Google Classroom, or other social-media platform for sharing resources and other information. Here are some other ways to use online platforms to build connections:

- **Share resources:** The facilitator and group members periodically share specific, relevant resources with the group.

- **Hold solution-oriented discussions:** The facilitator posts a challenge identified by the group and encourages members to offer solutions. He then monitors the discussion as needed.

- **Share teaching strategies:** Members share teaching strategies related to specific topics, such as ideas for including math and science learning in the preschool classroom.

- **Share videos:** Members post videos of themselves teaching and receive strengths-based feedback from other group members.

- **Arrange enrichment activities and fun:** Members post social events on the platform. Consider holding potlucks, celebrating members' birthdays, or even having a PLC session with a fun, creative theme. One PLC held a space-themed session called "Out-of-This-World Teaching." Another PLC had a detective-themed session called "The Case of the Missing Y."

It may help to offer multiple ways for members to contribute beyond face-to-face meetings.

MAINTAINING CONVERSATION FLOW

Sometimes the conversation lags during discussions. The facilitator supports the group by keeping the conversation moving with strategies such as these:

- Using open-ended questions
- Pausing and giving members time to think before they need to respond
- Inviting the group to help determine the learning agenda
- Asking group members if they are ready to shift to a new topic

The facilitator also maintains order in the discussion by reminding the group of protocols and climate-of-care guidelines. He remains impartial and sensitive to different viewpoints and creates a safe environment that promotes open dialogue among members.

KEYS TO EFFECTIVE PLCs

Many elements contribute to effective PLCs. Here are a few key points:

- Always keep your purpose, or *why*, as the central theme of each session.
- Focus on topics that help group members achieve that purpose.
- Be open to diverse viewpoints.
- Provide time for reflection and self-evaluation.
- Determine specific actions that group members can complete between sessions.
- Embed accountability measures within the PLC.

OVERCOMING COMMON CHALLENGES FOR PLCs

Forming and maintaining an effective PLC can be challenging. Here are some common obstacles that PLCs face and some ideas for overcoming them.

LACK OF ADMINISTRATIVE SUPPORT

In some organizations, the administration provides insufficient or inconsistent support for PLCs. For example, some administrators consider it financially prohibitive to bring child-care professionals together during work time. To overcome this type of obstacle, seek administrative support for your PLC before you organize it. Emphasize the benefits of PLCs, state the *why*, and share your PLC's focus and anticipated outcomes.

Case Study: Overcoming a Lack of Support

Melinda is the facilitator for a PLC of teachers at a child-care center. Although her administrators initially gave verbal support for forming the PLC, they are less supportive now that it is up and running. They question whether it is the best use of teachers' time to get together and talk.

Melinda schedules a meeting with the administrators to help them understand the benefits of the PLC. She collects photos and anecdotes from the teachers that demonstrate changes within their classrooms. When she meets with the administrators, she describes and shows how providing teachers with a forum to talk, create action plans, and problem solve is benefitting the children in the participants' classrooms. Surprised and pleased, the administrators resume their support for the PLC.

POOR GROUP LEADERSHIP

If PLCs are not organized or facilitated effectively, group members can have a negative experience. Without clear discussion protocols, PLCs may lose focus and turn into places for airing complaints. Group members with divergent views, strong personalities, and argumentative attitudes can also derail a PLC, especially with an unprepared or unskilled facilitator. Take time to find a skilled facilitator, or ensure that the selected facilitator receives sufficient training and support before beginning PLC sessions.

LACK OF LASTING CHANGE

Even when PLCs have productive conversations, those discussions still might not lead to changes in members' practices or in child outcomes. This may happen because the group members lose sight of the PLC's objectives or do not build accountability into the group processes. To avoid these problems, plan ahead, identify potential challenges, and develop strategies for addressing those difficulties.

Case Study: Laying the Groundwork for Lasting Change

Jordan has been asked to facilitate a new PLC for teachers at a preschool. She knows that several of the teachers have strong personalities and may be reluctant to fully participate, so she schedules a meeting with each teacher prior to the first PLC session. During these meetings, Jordan tells each teacher that she values the expertise that he can bring to the group, and she invites each teacher to give input on how he can strengthen the PLC. Jordan explains the proposed format and objectives of the PLC. She takes time to answer the teachers' questions and addresses their concerns. Finally, she asks for and receives a commitment from each teacher to take on a specific role to ensure the success of the PLC.

Case Study: My Experience in a PLC for Early Childhood Trainers

I have experienced PLCs both as a facilitator and as a group member. For example, at the office where I work, a PLC was formed for all staff involved in training early childhood professionals. This group, which is still meeting as of this writing, includes both seasoned and new trainers, and I serve as the facilitator.

Our PLC holds a two-hour meeting each month. Every session begins by having each trainer share a "glow" (something related to training that went well this month) and a "grow" (a training challenge or issue that the person faced during the month). After hearing a grow, all group members can offer strengths-based feedback and ideas to address the concern, including personal experiences with similar challenges. After this sharing, the group examines specific training practices.

During one of our past sessions, we read Carl Dunst's article "Improving the Design and Implementation of In-Service Professional Development in Early Childhood Intervention," which outlines seven key features of evidence-informed PL. The PLC members all create and carry out training sessions, so each person reflected on ways that he had or had not included Dunst's key features in a training session that he (the participant) had recently designed and implemented. Then we discussed strengths and challenges that we had discovered through this reflection. We collaboratively developed ideas for overcoming those challenges. As facilitator, I then challenged each trainer to design and implement a new training session using Dunst's key features and to report the results at the next meeting.

This PLC is effective because it focuses on current practices, requires members to take immediate action, and holds them accountable by having them report outcomes at subsequent sessions. See appendix B for more examples of topics and guiding questions for PLCs for trainers and coaches.

CONSIDERATIONS FOR STARTING YOUR PLC

If you are considering forming a PLC, consider these questions:

- What is our *why*, or shared purpose?

- What is our focus? (How will we meet the purpose expressed in our *why*?)

- How will we structure our sessions?

- Who will be the facilitator? What roles and responsibilities will he have?

- How will the facilitator cultivate strong group engagement?

- In what ways can the facilitator keep the PLC on task?

- How can the facilitator address group members' difficult behaviors?

- What types of evaluations should we conduct for our PLC?

- Would it help to survey potential members to determine interests, topics, availability, and preferred platforms?

CHAPTER 4:

Communities of Practice
in Early Childhood Education

Nevaeh, a child-care-center director, is participating in a CoP that focuses on leadership. At one of the recent sessions, the members discussed what it means to be a courageous leader. Among other things, they talked about how a courageous leader focuses on doing what is best for her organization, which can include letting staff go.

Nevaeh realizes that she needs to address the issues she is having with one of her staff members. Using suggestions from her CoP peers, she meets with this person and objectively and forthrightly states her concerns. She and the staff member mutually agree that this person should seek other employment.

This chapter describes how to create and implement CoPs. Some of the ideas for effective PLCs also apply to CoPs, but as mentioned earlier, the two groups have important differences. CoPs' purpose is to bring together groups of individuals from various organizations based on a shared interest, such as leadership. Participation in CoPs is voluntary, and their collaborative structure is often informal. The focus is on sharing knowledge, solving problems jointly, building relationships, and improving practices.

SETTING UP A CoP

Occasionally, CoPs form organically as members come together based on shared interests. In contrast, many CoPs form because a facilitator brings everyone together, organizes logistics, and takes the lead in communicating with members. Either way, when a CoP forms within a supportive organization, the organization can often provide physical space for meetings, offer technology expertise, or provide funding.

As a leader within your organization, you will likely serve as the driving force behind a CoP and become its facilitator. So how do you actually go about setting up a CoP? There are four main steps: determine interests, develop a group vision statement, establish peer learning teams, and build group connections.

CONDUCT A SURVEY TO DETERMINE INTERESTS

The recommendations in this chapter are based on my experiences facilitating CoPs, specifically one CoP focused on leadership. For some time, I had been providing monthly training for child-care-center directors in my area to help them improve practices at their centers. One director suggested forming a CoP about leadership and inviting additional directors to participate. The other participants liked the idea, and I was asked to facilitate the CoP.

First, the group wanted to assess potential participants' interests. With feedback from the group, I developed an online survey and emailed it to all the child-care-center directors in the area. The survey listed specific leadership and supervision topics and asked respondents to rate their interest in each on a scale from one (no interest) to three (lots of interest). The survey also included questions about the best meeting times, frequencies, and lengths.

The results showed that about twenty-five additional child-care-center directors wanted to participate in the CoP. They were invited to join the group, which (based on the survey results) would meet for two hours each month over a period of eight months. The most popular topics from the survey became eight main categories for the CoP to explore:

- The power of positive, engaged leadership

- Leading early childhood programs effectively

- Positive, strengths-based supervision

- Strengthening staff relationships

- Addressing staff challenges (such as turnover, gossip, conflicts, and burnout)

- Intentional PL and training staff

- Strategies for coaching and mentoring staff

- Fostering teamwork and collaboration with staff

Given these interests, the CoP secured funding to purchase two resource books for participants to read between sessions: *Leading Early Childhood Organizations* and *Developing People in Early Childhood Organizations*, both by Exchange Press. As facilitator, I developed and distributed a list of guiding questions for each session (see appendix C).

DEVELOP A GROUP VISION STATEMENT

Developing a group vision statement provides a focus for CoP members. What outcomes do they desire at the end of the CoP? How do they want the CoP to function?

In the initial session with the leadership CoP, members shared words and phrases that described our visions of coming together as leaders. We then worked on combining ideas into longer phrases to create possible vision statements. Eventually, we settled on this version:

"Empowering leaders to motivate and inspire action." Subsequently, we read the vision statement at the beginning of each session.

ESTABLISH PEER LEARNING TEAMS

In the leadership CoP, to promote conversations among members with different backgrounds, I strategically organized participants into small (in this case, five-member) peer learning teams. This way, participants could interact with peers who came from different types of organizations and had diverse backgrounds and viewpoints. These smaller groups also enabled team members to learn and share in a more personal way than they could with the full group.

While PLCs sometimes use small-group activities, peer learning teams are a crucial part of CoPs. The goals of these teams are to:

- build trusting relationships;

- deepen understanding;

- help learners be open to possibilities and multiple perspectives;

- help learners be present and learn from one another; and

- ensure equity.

To promote participation and learning in peer learning teams, members take on specific roles within those teams. The team members determine which member will take which role.

The primary role in these groups is the team facilitator. This position is similar to that of the CoP facilitator, except the team-facilitator position is temporary, functions only when members work in peer learning teams, and should rotate among team members. The team facilitator promotes participation, ensures equity, and keeps the group focused and moving along. She poses questions and makes comments to guide the group, helps to broaden the conversation, and summarizes the key points.

Other peer-learning-team roles can include these assignments:

- **Scribe:** Keeps a record of the group's conversations

- **Presenter:** Distills thoughts and ideas from the group and shares them with the rest of the CoP

- **Timekeeper:** Keeps track of time

- **Artist:** Creates pictures and graphics for presentations

- **Resource manager:** Obtains needed resources and materials for the team, such as paper and handouts, and makes sure that everything is cleaned up after team activities

- **Encourager:** Offers encouragement to all team members, promotes a positive team atmosphere, and helps everyone feel welcome and included

If a peer learning team does not have enough members to fill all these roles, the members can select the roles that best meet their needs. Members can even take multiple roles, if needed. The CoP facilitator should encourage members to rotate roles periodically.

Case Study: A Peer Learning Team in Action

Kayla is the director at a for-profit child-care center. Her peer learning team includes directors from a Montessori program, a faith-based child-care center, and a Head Start program. Learning about these programs has given Kayla new perspective on the challenges that other program leaders face. Not surprisingly, some issues are common to everyone on her peer learning team—for example, they all struggle to find and retain qualified staff. Several of Kayla's teammates are also involved in the state's quality initiative, and listening to their perspectives has given Kayla ideas for improving her own program.

BUILD CONNECTIONS WITHIN PEER LEARNING TEAMS

Members of peer learning teams need to connect with each other. Try this engagement strategy at your CoP's first meeting to promote relationship building among the newly minted teams.

Engagement Strategy: I Light Up . . .

Materials

1 index card per participant

pens or pencils

1. Have participants sit with their peer learning teams, and give each person an index card (and a pen or pencil, if needed).

2. Instruct everyone to respond to the following prompts on her index card. The responses can be about anything related to early childhood:

   • I light up about . . .

   • I want to . . .

   • I advocate for . . .

3. When everyone has finished, invite participants to share their answers with their teammates.

Engagement Strategy: Your Leadership Journey

To continue building connections among the members of the peer learning teams in the leadership CoP, we used a facilitator-guided activity called Your Leadership Journey to promote group connections. This exercise is adapted from a learning experience that I participated in at a PD forum with Anne Hensley, coauthor of *Inspiring Peak Performance: Competence, Commitment, and Collaboration.*

1. Have participants sit with their peer learning teams. Pass out the "Your Leadership Journey" handout (see appendix D).

2. Direct participants to reflect on five to six stepping stones or stumbling blocks along their leadership journeys. Stepping stones and stumbling blocks can include significant choices, events, people, and places.

3. Tell participants to fill in their handouts by writing their stepping stones and stumbling blocks on the stones, including their past, current, and future leadership plans in the applicable sections.

4. After everyone finishes, invite peer learning teams to share their leadership journeys, or just the parts they are comfortable sharing, with each other. Remind participants that while a person is speaking, the rest of her team listens silently.

5. Once everyone has shared, encourage team members to comment on what they heard and to discuss similarities among teammates.

RESPONSIBILITIES OF THE FACILITATOR

A CoP facilitator guides participants along their journey of discovery. Within a CoP, any member can act as group facilitator, or several members can share this role. As the members of the CoP usually come from many different organizations, it is essential that a single member facilitate communication, such as sending reminders about sessions and distributing resources.

Other facilitator responsibilities include overseeing the logistics for sessions, either in person or virtually. The facilitator, in collaboration with group members, creates a general outline for CoP sessions. It can include discussion questions and corresponding reading assignments, such as articles or books. The facilitator makes sure the meeting space is set up to promote the desired types of interactions, such as small-group discussions. As discussed earlier, the facilitator helps groups stay organized and focused both during and between meetings.

KEYS TO EFFECTIVE CoPs

Once your CoP is set up, it requires effort to maintain. Make these components part of your CoP to promote its success.

GROUP AUTONOMY

The facilitator must give the other participants autonomy to make group decisions. She may feel tempted to veto ideas that complicate logistics; however, the group process is the heart of a CoP and needs to be honored. Seeking ideas from the group can also lead to valuable new experiences. For example, if the facilitator invites other members to host meetings and help with logistics, the group could develop and implement a schedule of rotating host sites.

Something similar happened in the leadership CoP. Participants wanted to visit and tour different child-care centers to gain ideas for their own programs, so we brainstormed about how to accomplish these visits. One member suggested setting up a tour to visit several facilities on a designated day. Another member recommended having the CoP meet at a different child-care center each month, and most members preferred this option. We adjusted our schedule to incorporate the various new meeting places and the additional time needed for touring the facilities.

For our first session at a child-care center, we met at the building at 9:00 a.m. We held our regular two-hour meeting and then toured the facility. By that time, we observed less child engagement in activities and learning centers than we would have seen earlier in the day, because children were now either eating lunch or getting ready for nap time. A participant suggested that for future sessions, we should take our center tours before our CoP sessions so that everyone could better observe child engagement in the classrooms. The group concurred, and we revised the schedule again.

Because we honored the group process and made these changes, the group was empowered, as it directed the format of the meetings, and member participation increased. We looked forward to the tours, which promoted discussions about what we had seen and heard. More resources began to circulate among CoP members because during the tours, the child-care-center directors often provided us with sample resources and information about features of their programs. Several directors even volunteered to serve us either breakfast or lunch.

BUILDING WHOLE-GROUP CONNECTIONS

Earlier in this chapter, we discussed the importance of building connections within peer learning teams, but it is also important to build connections within the CoP as a whole. When participants feel comfortable interacting with all group members, these relationships provide support both within and outside of the group. These interactions also enlarge professional networks and provide opportunities for collaboration.

For example, in the leadership CoP, one member commented that attending the CoP had helped her manage the day-to-day challenges of being a child-care-center director. Her membership had shown her that she was not alone; she now knew that she could reach out to other members for support and guidance outside of CoP sessions. Another member shared that she probably would not have left a previous job as a child-care-center director if she had been involved in the leadership CoP earlier in her career. In that position, she had lacked support and opportunities to problem solve with other administrators, all of which caused her to doubt her abilities and seek employment elsewhere. Overall, the opportunities for networking and support among CoP members promoted sustained commitment to the group.

MEMBER COMMITMENT

CoPs benefit most when members consistently participate in sessions. Consistently meeting with professional peers builds relationships and increases individuals' knowledge reservoirs. Sustained interactions create momentum for improvement.

To promote consistent attendance, establish a commitment expectation for your CoP. For instance, when the leadership CoP was created, potential members completed an application that outlined the expectations for membership, including an attendance requirement. Each applicant had to commit to attend seven out of eight CoP sessions over a one-year span (once per month, except in December and over the summer). From the results of our earlier survey, we knew that this was a manageable time commitment. In return for pledging to attend consistently, CoP members received professional resource books related to the proposed session topics. At the end of the initial commitment, members could commit to another eight sessions or leave the group. Most members wanted to continue participation because they found value in being part of the CoP. This renewal also provided a convenient opportunity to recruit new group members yearly.

SHARED CONTENT FOCUS

A shared content focus means having all CoP members concentrate on a specific topic, such as strengthening staff relationships. To promote the shared content focus, you may wish to provide group members with applicable professional resource books. If the CoP does not have funding available, members can purchase their own books. For a list of potentially useful books for a CoP on leadership, see appendix E.

To ensure that group members come ready for productive discussions, the facilitator can assign readings and guiding questions before each session. This practice also helps quieter group members, who may be more willing to speak if they have some material already prepared. Additionally, reading assignments provide springboards for discussions and additional ideas for members to consider. To promote discussion of reading assignments at meetings, try using a variety of reading engagement strategies (see chapter 12).

In the first year of the leadership CoP, we secured funding to provide books for the participants. They were excited to receive meaningful professional resources that they could study and use even outside the CoP. The reading assignments also primed the pump for thoughtful discussions at each session. During the sessions, peer learning teams discussed the readings and how they applied to leadership in members' programs. As we began the second year of the CoP, the participants recommended new books to discuss. We compiled a list from their suggestions, had the group vote on their top choices, and purchased the most requested books. For both years, we distributed a list of suggested readings for each session (included in appendix C).

ACCOUNTABILITY

Accountability is important in a CoP. It helps motivate CoP members to take action in a timely manner and to move the work of the group forward. To promote accountability in the leadership CoP, each member selected an accountability partner—someone who would check in with the member between sessions to help her keep her commitments, and vice versa. Partners determined how often they wanted to interact and the best method of communication. For example, they might email or text each other weekly to share things they had done or read. Through this check-in system, partners encouraged each other to complete the reading assignments and attend the CoP sessions. This partnership also provided support and networking opportunities. You may wish to use this method in your own CoP.

PRODUCTIVE SCHEDULING

To have a productive schedule for your CoP, get participants' input about preferred days and times for meetings. Once the schedule is set up, be willing to change days and times if those changes meet the needs of most members.

Earlier in this chapter, we discussed how the leadership CoP's schedule changed based on input from the members. Once the changes were finalized, each session had two parts: a child-care-center tour and a CoP meeting. Here is the schedule of the types of activities in the CoP meetings (not all activities were used every time). You can use these ideas as a model for your own CoP sessions:

- **Welcome and sharing of vision statement**
- **Peer learning team discussion:** "What did you do to grow as a leader this month?" (Remember, this CoP met monthly.)
- **Team discussion on assigned readings and guiding questions:** For example, at our session titled "Intentional Professional Learning: Training Staff," teams discussed this question: "How could you develop intentional, embedded PL opportunities for staff?"
- **Presentations by facilitator and group members:** This segment often included video clips and learning activities.
- **Think tanks**: Peer learning team members identified challenges and issues related to the day's topic that they wanted to discuss. Then members left their teams and grouped with other participants who wanted to discuss similar topics. These smaller groups eventually coalesced into three to four think-tank discussion groups, each led by the person who had identified the chosen discussion topic. Depending on the interests of the group, this process could be repeated to discuss additional ideas.
- **Case studies and scenarios:** Peer learning teams discussed case studies and scenarios related to the day's topic.
- **Reflection time:** Members reflected on their current practices and developed plans for growing as leaders in the month ahead.

OVERCOMING COMMON CHALLENGES FOR CoPs

One difficulty for CoPs is maintaining members' long-term interest in participating. Time is a limited commodity, and many different demands compete for members' time. For instance, occasionally participants in my leadership CoP could not attend sessions thanks to last-minute emergencies at their child-care centers. Sometimes these situations are unavoidable, but one of the goals of the leadership CoP was to help directors deepen the leadership pools at their centers so other people could also handle emergencies. We found that to maintain members' interest, we had to ensure that they felt the value in attending sessions and had opportunities to discuss meaningful topics with other professionals.

Members' behavior during sessions can also cause problems for CoPs. As we have discussed previously, a strong facilitator can alleviate many of these situations. Also, because CoP membership is voluntary, typically only genuinely motivated participants attend. Obtaining regular feedback from members can help you identify which components are (not) working. To increase buy-in and thereby promote higher levels of attendance at sessions, try having the members determine the discussion topics and providing professional resources, such as books, to refer to for each session.

Case Study: Bringing Together Diverse Groups of Coaches

In my community, there are five ongoing early childhood initiatives that include coaching as a component of PL. At one time, many child-care programs in the community each had two or more coaches working with their staffs. Some teachers felt confused and overwhelmed by all the initiatives, and some directors and teachers began resisting coaching because they were receiving conflicting information from different initiatives.

To establish greater collaboration in the coaching community, I invited the coaches from all five initiatives to a meeting. We exchanged information about the different initiatives and created a resource list with all the coaches' names, their contact information, and whom they were coaching. Coaches committed that if teachers or directors complained about receiving conflicting information from different initiatives, the coaches would contact each other to discuss the issue.

This group also decided to establish a coaching CoP and meet quarterly to learn about common coaching challenges and strengths-based practices. Members from each initiative agreed to facilitate a session. At sessions, coaches gave updates on their initiatives, shared successes and challenges, and discussed topics of interest in small groups. This CoP helped the coaches establish a strong support network and a more unified approach to PL within the community.

CONSIDERATIONS FOR STARTING YOUR CoP

If you are interested in forming a CoP, consider these questions:

- What is our area of focus? Is that topic current and relevant?

- What is our purpose, or desired outcome?

- Whom will we invite to join the CoP? How can we bring people with diverse perspectives into the group? Remember, membership is voluntary. Invite more people than you think you need to; not everyone will participate.

- What type of time commitment works best for potential members? The leadership CoP, as we have seen, met for two hours each month. Some virtual CoPs meet for one hour every other month. Be realistic about time commitments, especially if group members live far away or in different time zones. Professionals have many demands for their time.

- Can we meet face-to-face, or should we meet virtually to include more members from diverse locations?

- Would it help to survey potential members to determine interests, topics, availability, and preferred platforms?

PART 2

MENTORING
AND
COACHING

CHAPTER 5:

Mentoring

Sandra has almost completed her bachelor's degree in early childhood education. One of the requirements is for her to complete an internship focused on child-care administration. Megan, the assistant director of the child-care center where Sandra will intern, will serve as her mentor. At their first meeting, Megan explains that she and Sandra will meet twice a week and focus on Sandra's individual development as a manager. Sandra wants to learn how to effectively supervise staff, so Megan guides her in creating some goals based on this interest.

As Sandra works on her goals, she hits some roadblocks. She struggles to complete all her daily tasks and has difficulties with a teacher who refuses to listen to anything an intern has to say. At the next meeting, Sandra explains her concerns to Megan, who offers advice on time management and dealing with difficult employees.

WHAT IS MENTORING?

Mentoring is the practice of having a professional with more experience, education, and expertise in a specific field (a *mentor*) provide guidance and support to a less-experienced professional (a *mentee*). Mentoring focuses on enhancing the individual development of a mentee, who is often a student or new employee. Mentors also guide mentees through challenging situations in and around the workplace. For example, a mentor could help a mentee learn to navigate and understand an organization's culture, become proficient in skills that are part of a new job, resolve a conflict with a coworker, or determine the best strategies to help a child with challenging behavior. The mentor's guidance decreases the amount of time needed for the mentee to acclimate to a new work environment.

A successful mentoring relationship empowers a mentee and gives him the courage to be and do things he might not have thought possible. Mentors guide mentees to see themselves in new ways and recognize their future potential. Therefore, mentors should be carefully selected.

Because you may be interested in being a mentor, a mentee, or both, we will discuss both aspects of mentoring in this chapter.

BENEFITS OF MENTORING

Aside from those already mentioned, mentoring provides other important benefits. Mentors direct mentees to professional resources and people. Mentors also help mentees understand the current challenges and trends within a community. Even an experienced professional can profit from mentoring.

My own experience with mentoring illustrates some of these benefits. When I was a new faculty member at a university, I had two mentors. The first was a tenured faculty member who had many connections within the early childhood field and introduced me to key partners in the community. She also met with regularly me to discuss the steps I needed to take to receive tenure. Her experience, wisdom, and guidance were invaluable, particularly for the teaching and programming side of my position. Her assistance helped me keep my professional priorities in order. My second mentor was a faculty member with extensive expertise in developing research, securing grants, and writing professional publications, and her guidance helped me hone these important skills. We also developed a close personal friendship.

Mentoring relationships can change or end over time, such as when one party moves into a new position or leaves the organization. Though I no longer work with my first two mentors, their influence still shapes my professional practice, and I have benefitted from working with additional mentors throughout my career. My current mentor, for instance, has expertise in developing and conducting program evaluations, and his assistance has been priceless in helping me cultivate these abilities.

ESTABLISHING SUCCESSFUL MENTORING RELATIONSHIPS

Clearly, mentoring is a powerful form of PL. So how do you begin a mentoring relationship? Some organizations have formal mentoring programs for their employees, in which case you may be assigned as a mentor or mentee. In other cases, the mentee selects a mentor, or vice versa. Because a mentor's work is so involved and usually takes place in addition to his regular workload, a mentor typically only has one mentee, or possibly two, at a time.

CHOOSING (TO BE) A MENTOR

If you are looking for a mentor, follow these steps:

1. Identify areas in your professional life (or in those of your staff) that need growth and development. For example, many early childhood professionals seek mentoring in time management, conflict resolution, or classroom management.

2. Identify individuals who could serve as potential mentors.

3. Meet with each person one-on-one to discuss your ideas and the types of information and support you hope to gain from the relationship.

4. Determine which mentoring relationship is most desirable and feasible. (It is easiest to start with one mentor. We will discuss having multiple mentors later.)

5. Reach out to your selected mentor, and, if that person agrees, establish the details of your mentoring relationship.

6. If you are approached about being a mentor, consider these important factors before giving your answer:

   • Are you interested in being a mentor?

   • Do you have the time to be an effective mentor?

   • Does your expertise match the needs of the mentee?

If you answered yes to all three questions, the next step is to consider the characteristics of effective mentors.

Characteristics of Effective Mentors

Remember, successful mentoring relationships do not just happen. They are based on several key components. If you are considering being a mentor, reflect on your ability to embody the following characteristics. If you are choosing a mentor, look for these qualities and behaviors:

• **Compatibility:** The goals and expectations of the mentor and mentee need to align. The mentor should have strengths that match the mentee's needs.

• **Trustworthiness:** No relationship, particularly a mentoring one, can survive without trust. It is built over time through respectful interactions.

• **Candid communication:** A mentor's job is not to simply validate what a mentee is doing. Mentors need to be honest and open about mentees' progress. Mentors should candidly challenge mentees' ideas and encourage mentees to grow.

• **Active listening:** Active listening is seeking to hear and understand the meaning of what is being said. Both mentors and mentees need to actively listen. This is more than hearing the words; it is also understanding the emotions behind the words.

• **Openness:** Both mentors and mentees must be willing to try new ways of doing things and to think about information from diverse perspectives. In particular, mentors need to be open to their mentees' viewpoints.

• **Innovation:** Mentoring requires taking risks and being innovative. Amazing things happen when individuals step outside their comfort zones.

• **Collaboration:** Mentors and mentees work together toward mutual goals for mentees' development.

• **Organization:** The roles and responsibilities of both mentors and mentees need to be clearly defined. For example, who keeps track of any required paperwork? If the mentor and mentee disagree about a decision, who has the final say? Mentoring relationships should also specify how and when the parties will communicate so that everyone knows what to expect and can follow through.

• **Vision:** Mentors help mentees see themselves both as they are and as they can be. Mentors also provide actionable steps that guide mentees in turning their visions into reality.

- **Developing and accomplishing goals:** Mentors assist mentees in establishing achievable goals. Mentors then monitor mentees' progress and celebrate their accomplishments.

- **Gratitude:** Both parties benefit from interacting with and learning from each other. Mentees should thank mentors for their time and advice. Mentors should thank mentees for their willingness to develop professionally.

Case Study: Lucinda's Mentor

Lucinda wants to learn how to obtain funding for a literacy program at her child-care center. She has asked Alex, a successful grant writer, to mentor her in creating a funding proposal for a local foundation. Alex listens attentively to Lucinda's ideas and helps her understand what kind of project is realistic and fundable. Together, they develop a plan of action. Alex also gives Lucinda the contact information of several people to talk to about her ideas.

Lucinda starts to develop her proposal based on Alex's feedback. As they continue to meet, he asks hard questions and pushes her to do more research on her ideas. He suggests ways to present a compelling argument and create an appropriate budget.

After several months, Lucinda and her community partners present their proposal to the foundation's board. The board is impressed by their preparation. Lucinda and her partners are awarded the funding.

As you can see from this example, mentors are effective when they:

- stretch their mentees' abilities;

- keep feedback clear and concise;

- ask probing questions that help mentees discover solutions to problems; and

- remain flexible and open-minded.

Having Multiple Mentors

In an article for Inside Higher Ed, Kerry Ann Rockquemore discusses a common misconception about mentoring: that one "guru" can meet all a mentee's needs. In fact, mentees often benefit from having multiple mentors to shape different aspects of their professional journeys.

Receiving professional advice from different people provides diverse perspectives and guidance. Remember, even good mentors do not always give perfect advice. You may wish to discuss ideas with several mentors to determine the best course of action. If this exercise produces conflicting advice, try consulting a neutral party, such as a trusted colleague who can offer an objective perspective. However, ultimately you must choose your own route to success. You might simply have to select a path, begin, and adjust along the way.

STRUCTURING YOUR PARTNERSHIP

Once you have chosen a mentor, what details do you need to establish about your relationship? That depends on your individual goals and circumstances, including any requirements you must meet as part of a formal mentoring program. However, all successful mentoring relationships involve at least these steps:

1. Set up a schedule for regular communication. Mentoring tends to be more time intensive at the beginning of a relationship. You and your mentor might choose to meet in person, talk on the phone, email, or video chat. These sessions may be formal or informal and can happen daily, weekly, monthly, or as needed.

2. Document your progress along the way. Keep track of your goals and the steps required to meet each. For example, you could create a written action plan and check off each step as you complete it.

3. Continue to network with other potential mentors, as needed. Even the best mentor cannot teach you everything you need to know.

As you begin working with your mentor, remember that mentoring is a partnership. We all have expertise to share. As you communicate with a potential mentor, you may find that you have skills and abilities that would benefit him. For instance, you could share your technological expertise with a mentor who is not as technologically savvy. The benefits of mentoring can flow in both directions.

Case Study: The Emerging Leader and Mentoring (ELM) Program

I have experienced the benefits of mentoring not only as a mentee but also as a mentor. For several years, I participated in the Emerging Leader and Mentoring (ELM) Program, a formal mentoring arrangement sponsored by my local Association for the Education of Young Children (AEYC) board. The program sought to mentor emerging leaders in the early childhood field to grow new leaders for the association's board and the local early-childhood community. Each year, program facilitators invited early childhood professionals to apply to participate as either mentors or emerging leaders. The application included questions on areas of interest, and the program's facilitators used this information to pair each mentor with one or two emerging leaders.

The ELM Program took place over an eight-month period. Each emerging leader had an ongoing assignment to develop and implement a project that would increase his leadership skills and benefit the early-childhood community. Both mentors and emerging leaders also attended PL sessions, which were held once per month for three hours. The first two hours featured training on specific leadership topics. During the third hour, mentors and emerging leaders met and discussed the training topic and the emerging leaders' projects.

One of my mentees in this program was a child-care-center director whom I'll call Dara. For her leadership project, she wanted to create a brochure about inclusive practices for the families of the children at her center. For six months, Dara and I discussed the current inclusion practices at her center, ideas for strengthening those practices, resources already available to families, and resources that Dara could use to develop her brochure. When she created her first draft, I reviewed it and provided feedback.

After several more discussions and revisions, the brochure was ready. Dara had it printed and distributed it to families. Additionally, she held a parent night at her center to talk about inclusion and discuss the brochure. Dara later told me that she received a lot of positive feedback from families about her project and that she wanted to continue providing them with information on inclusion.

Other emerging leaders have completed a variety of projects within the ELM Program. For instance, one person collected book donations to start a lending library for parents at a Head Start center. Another person created a training session on advocacy that was presented at her state's early childhood conference. A third person collected donations to purchase cot sheets for a child-care center in a community with limited resources.

The ELM Program has borne many positive fruits for everyone involved. Family members and children in the community received increased access to books, sheets to sleep on at nap time, and other benefits. The mentors had opportunities to make positive differences in the lives of the emerging leaders by nurturing and guiding their growth and development. The emerging leaders developed important relationships, cultivated skills, and exchanged expertise with their mentors. Additionally, some emerging leaders were invited to present poster sessions on their projects at our state's early childhood conference. Several program graduates have become board members and officers of local and state AEYC groups.

SETTING UP AN ELM PROGRAM

If you would like to establish an ELM Program in your area, follow these steps:

1. Identify and secure sponsors and facilitators for the program.

2. Develop the program's structure and schedule, including an orientation meeting, monthly PL sessions, and a culminating event.

3. Create an application and invite early childhood professionals in your area to apply to be either emerging leaders or mentors.

4. Using the application results, pair emerging leaders and mentors based on interests.

5. Have a welcome event to introduce the program. Include time for the emerging leaders and mentors to socialize and start building relationships.

6. Provide monthly PL sessions on leadership topics for emerging leaders and mentors. Include time for them to discuss projects and other topics of concern.

7. Arrange a culminating event for the emerging leaders to showcase their final projects.

8. All along the way, celebrate the development of each emerging leader.

MENTORING YOUR STAFF

If you are a supervisor, you may have opportunities to mentor your own staff, particularly if they are new to your program. To begin the process, meet with each mentee and discuss his strengths, interests, and professional goals. Ideally, this meeting happens soon after an employee joins your organization, but you can have similar meetings with longtime employees. For example, as a supervisor of trainers and coaches, I hold periodic mentoring conversations with my staff but meet more frequently with new staff. In each meeting, we discuss that staff member's individual development and big dreams. Over the years, I have learned that several staff members dreamed of completing bachelor's or master's degrees in early childhood education. By being flexible with these staff members' work hours to accommodate their class schedules, we have all benefited: they have been able to both work and attend school, and I have retained long-term and increasingly qualified employees. I even served as one staff member's advisor for a professional internship. This experience demonstrates an important principle: by helping your employees develop, you strengthen your program.

KEYS TO SUCCESS

As you mentor your staff, keep these important practices in mind:

- Encourage staff members who want to pursue advanced degrees or specialized training.

- If possible, be flexible with work schedules to accommodate college classes or specialized training courses.

- Show interest in employees' professional pursuits, and take time to discuss what they have been learning.

- Set up opportunities for staff to give presentations to their colleagues about what they are learning.

- Learn more about employees' professional goals. Support the pursuit of those goals, even if it means some staff will leave your employment after achieving them.

This last key may surprise you. Why would you support something that could cause you to lose a staff member? It helps to take a holistic view and think about how the early childhood field as a whole—not just your program—will benefit from this employee's talents, abilities, and enhanced education. For example, one of my staff members (whom I'll call Joselyn) wanted to become involved with the Play, Policy, and Practice Interest Forum of the National Association for the Education of Young Children (NAEYC). This forum raises awareness of the need for play in early childhood. I encouraged Joselyn's interest, and she arranged for key people from the forum to present at our state's early-childhood conference. Shortly thereafter, Joselyn moved out of state for other employment opportunities. Although I lost her as a staff member, her professional growth positively affected her career path and, in addition, influenced many other early childhood professionals.

REMEMBER TO CHECK IN REGULARLY

To mentor your staff effectively, you need to stay aware of their successes and challenges. You can hold these check-ins during regular mentoring sessions or as separate activities. For example, I ask my staff to complete a simple reflection form each month. It contains prompts like these:

- Summarize your activities from this month.

- Share a highlight from your activities.

- Share any challenges or concerns.

- List your future plans or other comments or questions you have (optional).

The responses to each of these statements may be short or lengthy, depending on the staff member and the activities of the month. This form helps me acknowledge and recognize employees and learn about their challenges and concerns. Sometimes the responses reveal that I need to address certain issues, but most of the time, the staff simply explain how they handled their difficulties and what happened as a result. This information helps me be proactive and identify potential issues early so I can give extra encouragement and support or seek more information about specific situations. Of course, not all challenges or concerns can wait until the end of the month. If an urgent need or complex problem arises, I encourage the affected staff member to meet with me as soon as possible.

I have found that being a mentor is a rewarding experience. I find joy in watching others improve their abilities and do and become more than they once thought was possible. Mentors are an essential component to growing the early childhood profession.

CHAPTER 6:

Introduction to Coaching

Tabitha, a toddler teacher, has just begun working with a coach named Erica. During their first coaching session, Erica and Tabitha review and sign a coach-teacher partnership agreement that outlines their respective responsibilities. As they work together, Erica focuses on Tabitha's strengths and emerging skills and offers new strategies for Tabitha's classroom. By being willing to reflect on her teaching and try new ideas, Tabitha has grown as a teacher. Coaching has helped her gain greater confidence in her abilities: not only does she feel connected to the children, but she has noticed a difference in their behavior as well.

WHAT IS COACHING?

The last chapter discussed mentoring, a form of PL that focuses on encouraging individual development. In contrast, within an educational setting, coaching is a form of on-the-job, ongoing PL designed to help teachers acquire, enhance, or refine specific teaching skills. While mentoring guides teachers through a variety of issues, coaching primarily seeks to empower teachers to make positive changes in their teaching practices. To that end, coaching involves regular coaching sessions, which commonly have two parts:

1. A coaching observation, which the coach conducts in the teacher's classroom

2. A coaching conversation, in which the teacher and the coach create action plans for improving practices

Table 6.1: Mentoring versus Coaching summarizes the main differences between mentoring and coaching.

Table 6.1: Mentoring versus Coaching

	Mentoring	Coaching
OVERVIEW	Experienced person (mentor) provides guidance and support to less-experienced individual (mentee)	Person with specific expertise or skills (coach) helps others (often teachers) develop skills
FOCUS	Development Guiding mentee toward personal and professional growth Teaching mentee how to navigate work culture and relationships	Performance Helping teachers acquire new skills and practices Enhancing teachers' overall performance Improving child outcomes
STRUCTURE	Usually informal, sometimes formal Ongoing, longer-term relationship	Usually formal Relationship lasts for a specified time period
MEETINGS	Long-term career and personal development Increased personal and professional capacity	Achieving specific skill- and practice-related goals set by teacher and coach (and possibly administrator) Improved job performance Improved child outcomes

BENEFITS OF COACHING

Coaching provides teachers with one-on-one support designed to help them improve their interactions and classroom environments. Coaches differentiate their coaching to meet the individual needs of each teacher. Many coaching initiatives also provide teachers with materials for their classrooms. As coaching positively affects teaching practices, child outcomes often improve.

Coaching has become a much more common practice in the early childhood field than it once was. Many early-childhood quality initiatives, such as the Quality Rating Improvement System (QRIS), include coaching as a key component to improve the caliber of child care. Coaching initiatives also constitute important parts of other projects focused on building literacy, fostering social-emotional development, and improving teacher-child interactions. Whether your organization implements coaching as part of a specific project or as a standalone program, coaching benefits both teachers and coaches.

One teacher referred to coaching as having a "guide by the side." Indeed, even though a coach typically is assigned to multiple teachers at a time, she meets one-on-one with each person. Coaching becomes a collaborative partnership as the coach and the teacher establish trust, develop mutual goals, and reach agreed-upon outcomes.

Coaches play the role of cheerleaders by rooting for the home team. They encourage and support teachers by modeling best practices and helping them create plans of action. They facilitate sustainable change and remind teachers to act on their ideas for improvement.

CHARACTERISTICS OF EFFECTIVE COACHES

Coaching is a complex process, as each teacher and each coach brings distinct characteristics to the partnership. Therefore, administrators must choose coaches wisely. Though every coach will have a unique approach to her work, effective coaches share many of the following qualities.

KNOWLEDGE

Effective coaches have thorough knowledge of early childhood. They have worked as early childhood teachers, so they understand how children develop and learn and can empathize with the challenges that teachers face. They keep abreast of current research in the educational field and know how to implement evidence-based teaching practices in the classroom.

Equally important, effective coaches understand adult learning. They deeply comprehend adult learning principles and human psychology and know how to facilitate behavioral change. They also have strong foundations in the subjects or techniques they coach, such as language and literacy instruction, and understand the cultures of the programs in which they work. Effective coaches have previously worked with adult learners and know that people communicate and learn in a variety of ways. After all, teachers have a vast range of educational backgrounds, teaching experience, and PL needs, as do coaches. Therefore, effective coaches can differentiate and respond to the individual needs of each teacher. These coaches facilitate teacher reflection and respond appropriately to teachers' openness or resistance to coaching.

LEADERSHIP SKILL

Effective coaches are positive and proactive. They actively listen and communicate ideas clearly. They manage their time, plan, organize, and multitask when needed. Not only do they have a vision of what needs to be accomplished, but they share and develop that vision with the teachers they coach. Effective coaches know their priorities. They focus on bringing about successful outcomes for children by strengthening teachers, and they encourage each teacher to move forward at her own pace.

PERSONALITY TRAITS

Effective coaches have distinct personality traits that contribute to their success. If you are a coach but have not yet mastered all these attributes, take heart. You can develop them.

Unassuming

Unassuming coaches are genuine and selfless. They realize that coaching is not about them—it is about the teachers and the children. Unassuming coaches do not feel the need to share all their knowledge and skills with teachers, because they know that teachers grow more by developing their own knowledge and skills. To this end, unassuming coaches serve as guides. They meet teachers where they are and support them in enhancing their teaching practices.

Nurturing

Nurturing coaches are reliable, supportive, and trustworthy. They care about teachers as both professionals and people, so they take time to become acquainted with teachers and help teachers feel safe enough to share what is working and not working in their classrooms. Nurturing coaches are nonjudgmental, patient, and persistent. By providing positive, strengths-based feedback, they encourage teachers to change practices and to try new instructional strategies.

Respectful

Respectful coaches honor the space and interactions that take place in the classrooms of the teachers they coach. In other words, instead of immediately telling teachers what to change, respectful coaches seek to learn the reasons why teachers choose to set up their environments and interact with the children in particular ways. These coaches carefully listen to teachers' thoughts and suggestions, defer to their expertise, and emphasize teachers' goals rather than pushing their own objectives. Respectful coaches assist teachers in problem solving, exploring what teachers are doing successfully and what they might want to do differently. Together, teachers and respectful coaches define what success looks like and what resources they need to achieve it. These coaches keep confidences and share relevant strengths-based information (such as coaching goals and teachers' progress toward them) only with those who need to know, such as supervisors. Coaches do not snitch to administrators (which we further discuss later in this chapter).

Adaptable

Adaptable coaches adjust their approaches to meet the unique needs of each teacher and address the different situations that arise during coaching. They recognize and acknowledge the small changes that teachers make, even when progress seems slow, and remember that new habits take time to develop. Adaptable coaches try various methods until they learn the best ways to interact with each teacher.

Credible

Credible coaches are reliable and realistic. They have worked as early childhood teachers themselves, so they understand the challenges that teachers face in the classroom. Teachers benefit from watching credible coaches model best practices with the children in the teachers' classrooms. Coaches can then support teachers in implementing those same practices. Credible coaches acknowledge that they do not have all the answers, and they collaborate with teachers to seek information.

Approachable

Approachable coaches are easy to talk to and friendly, not aloof, distant, or physically remote. They dress appropriately. Not only are they open and responsive to teachers' ideas, but they take the time to be active listeners and really hear what teachers seek to share. Approachable coaches use acronyms and unfamiliar terms with caution, striving for clear and concise language. When these coaches show enthusiasm about the positive aspects of teachers' classrooms, teachers respond optimistically. (**Note:** Even when a coach is naturally approachable, it helps if she serves in a non-evaluative role—that is, she is not the immediate supervisor of the teachers she coaches, does not have the power to fire them, and does not perform their annual evaluations. This dynamic helps teachers feel more comfortable coming to their coaches for assistance.)

Accessible

Accessible coaches are easy to reach in person and through phone calls, emails, or texts. They are willing to have informal discussions with teachers outside of structured coaching sessions. They respond to teachers' requests and provide answers and information in a timely manner.

Collaborative

Collaborative coaches work with teachers to solve problems and develop a shared vision. They are open to teachers' ideas and choices. Collaborative coaches focus on partnership, striving to form a team with each teacher they coach. They guide teachers through the problem-solving process in a collaborative manner by being slow to offer solutions and quick to help teachers find answers within themselves.

Reflective

Reflective coaches ponder and study issues and encourage teachers to do the same. They ask specific questions that promote deep, careful thought, and then they give teachers time to think and reflect upon their teaching. Reflective coaches focus on understanding the thoughts and perceptions of the individuals they coach. They seek insights about each teacher and her unique situation and personality.

Case Study: An Effective Coach

Destiny has been coaching early childhood teachers for five years. When she first starts working with a teacher, she asks the teacher to draw an image of what she thinks is important for an effective coach-teacher partnership. One teacher, Gabriella, drew pictures that represented open feedback, collaboration, and encouragement. Then Destiny and Gabriella discussed what each of these elements would look like within a coaching relationship.

During coaching sessions, Destiny focuses on providing Gabriella with objective feedback. She respectfully asks Gabriella to share her ideas and encourages her to take risks and try new teaching strategies in her classroom. If something does not work out as planned, Destiny helps Gabriella reflect on what happened and what she could do differently next time. Destiny models practices and shares examples from when she was a classroom teacher. She notices even the small changes that Gabriella makes and encourages her to continue to stretch her abilities. Gabriella feels supported and is blossoming as her confidence in her abilities increases.

ESTABLISHING SUCCESSFUL COACHING PARTNERSHIPS

Coaches play a key role in establishing successful coaching partnerships. At the beginning of a coaching relationship, teachers sometimes assume that they are receiving coaching because they are doing something wrong or because they are not good teachers. But I like to remind teachers that even the world's best athletes have coaches. Just as athletes continually strive to become faster and more skilled in their sports, teachers should continually strive to improve the effectiveness of their teaching. In both athletics and education, coaches observe and assess skills and abilities so they can guide individuals to improve their performance.

DEFINE CLEAR ROLES, RESPONSIBILITIES, AND EXPECTATIONS

A coach and a teacher work most effectively as a team rather than as an expert and a novice. Within the partnership, the coach has expertise about teaching practices, and the teacher has expertise about her classroom and students. As a team, they can enhance positive outcomes for children. For this type of partnership to succeed, all the people involved need to understand their duties and what is expected of them.

Administrators and Coaches

Prior to meeting with a teacher for the first time, a coach should meet with the teacher's administrator to discuss what the coaching process will entail. The coach outlines her priorities and shares her vision for coaching. During the meeting, the coach and the administrator determine how and how often they will communicate (such as emailing each other twice a month). They also discuss the resources available or needed and the best ways for the administrator to be involved in the coaching partnership.

As mentioned earlier, coaching works best if the coach is in a non-evaluative position in relationship to the teacher. A teacher often becomes more open and willing to take risks if she knows her coach is not there to evaluate her. Therefore, the coach should make it clear that she will not spy for the administrator, although the coach will share updates on the teacher's progress. The coach's role is to support the teacher, build a trusting relationship, and collaborate with her to enhance teaching practices. The administrator's role is to provide the teacher with additional positive feedback and encouragement in meeting her goals.

Coaches and Teachers

Coaches often play a variety of roles, including serving as resources and supports for teachers, modeling direct instruction, and collecting and sharing assessment data. Teachers will need clarity about these roles, especially if they have never had a coach before. When a coach and a teacher have their first meeting, they should go over the roles and responsibilities of each person. The coach explains the desired outcomes and the expectations of the coaching program, including how she and the administrator will be involved. Likewise, the teacher shares what she would like to gain from coaching and any concerns she has about it.

Once both the teacher and the coach understand how the coaching process will work, they sign an agreement that clearly outlines the terms of the partnership. Having a written document helps alleviate teachers' concerns because it provides a permanent record of exactly what to expect. See appendix F for an example of a teacher-coach partnership agreement.

ADDRESS TEACHERS' CONCERNS

Teachers sometimes have concerns at the beginning of a coaching partnership. Here are some examples (using fictional names): Chun felt that coaching would take too much time. Ezinne did not think coaching would benefit her because she had years of teaching experience. Lotte, a new teacher, resented being coached, as she felt that she had not had any say in whether she participated in the coaching program. These types of feelings can hinder the coaching experience.

A coach can overcome these types of difficulties by encouraging a teacher to share her concerns at the start of a coaching partnership. Once the coach understands the problem, she can acknowledge and address it so that it does not fester. For instance, Chun began to discover that the strategies she learned during coaching actually decreased the amount of time she needed to spend handling challenging behaviors in her classroom. Ezinne was surprised to find out that her coach valued her expertise and asked her to share effective strategies with other teachers. Ezinne also found that by enhancing a few of her teaching techniques, she was reviving her enthusiasm for teaching. Lotte appreciated how her coach listened to her concerns, respectfully validated her feelings, honored her abilities, and worked as her partner to determine the specific goals they would work on.

Generally, as the coaching partnership progresses, teachers will see the benefits of the time spent in coaching. Often, even experienced teachers become more open to enhancing their teaching, and resentment is replaced by acceptance.

DEVELOP A TRUSTING RELATIONSHIP

Coaching can sometimes evoke uncomfortable feelings in both teachers and coaches. Teachers may feel judged and vulnerable when they know that someone is observing their teaching. In turn, coaches might hesitate to share assessment data (especially if it is less than favorable) or to interact with certain teachers, fearing a negative reception. These factors hamper the development of trust. However, trust is essential to a successful coaching experience. One of the desired outcomes of coaching is to help teachers identify their own strengths and determine opportunities for growth, but these discoveries usually do not happen unless teachers and coaches are willing to trust and be vulnerable with each other.

How can coaches address these challenges? Here are some simple techniques:

- Keep confidences.

- Begin coaching sessions with brief personal updates.

- Explain what you will do, and then do it.

- Notice the teacher's strengths and tell her what she is doing well.

A teacher needs to feel respected, supported, and valued in the coaching partnership. Effective coaches maintain confidentiality, respect teachers' expertise, and communicate effectively to build trust. Trust also grows as teachers and coaches collaborate and acknowledge that they both have expertise to share with each other. For example, during a coaching session, one teacher told her coach that she (the teacher) had developed a system for organizing the materials for her small-group times. The coach was excited to see this system and asked if she could take a picture of it and share it with other teachers. The teacher was pleased that the coach thought that something the teacher had created would be of value to other teachers. If you are a coach and see a great idea in a teacher's classroom, learn more about it and ask the teacher if you can share it with others.

Coaches build partnerships with teachers by noticing the little things that happen in their classrooms. One coach commented that it was her job to point out to teachers how their actions affected the children. She would tell teachers things such as, "Did you notice how the children responded when you told the story *Caps for Sale* using props and actions? They were excited and eager to actively participate," or "Did you see how the children hurried and cleaned up their toys so they could come over to the carpet and join you in the freeze dance? They didn't need any extra reminders; they knew what to do."

Trust increases when the content of coaching clearly connects to the teacher's everyday responsibilities. During the coaching partnership, the coach and the teacher examine current practices, focus on building skills and competencies, and plan for future practices. These activities should happen regularly, connect to what the teacher does every day, and deeply examine what does and does not work. If, on the other hand, coaching sessions are held sporadically, focus on material that does not relate to current needs, or only superficially explore topics, teachers will feel that their time is being wasted. Similarly, coaching should help teachers practice, reflect, and change their practices within an encouraging, supportive environment. Ridicule, criticism, and unreasonable expectations destroy trust.

Coaches also build trust by listening and learning why teachers do what they do. Coaches should avoid making snap judgments based on their own preferences and biases. For instance, if a coach believes that older infants should have opportunities to feed themselves, she may react with concern to seeing a teacher feed the older infants in a classroom. But the reasons behind teachers' actions may not be what they seem. Perhaps the teacher feeds the infants because of parental requests or program policies. Coaches build trust when they ask questions and seek to understand why instead of assuming and criticizing. The reasons why teachers do what they do are often surprising. When you understand why, you can frame your response based on what you learn.

For example, I saw a teacher whom I coached using what I considered to be a developmentally inappropriate behavior chart. When I asked her about the chart, she stated that she knew some kindergarten teachers who were using a similar chart, so she was using her chart to prepare the children in her class for kindergarten. This exchange told me that preparing children for kindergarten was important to this teacher. I asked her if she was open to learning other guidance techniques that could help the children gain the self-regulation skills they needed for kindergarten. She said that she was, and working from that angle, we were able to replace the behavior chart with other behavior-guidance strategies. The outcome would have been much different if I had immediately told this teacher that the behavior chart was developmentally inappropriate and that she needed to discard it. Those actions would have destroyed trust and would not have helped her understand why another method was better for helping children develop self-regulation skills.

There is power in building relationships with teachers. For instance, I supervise coaches in a program for infant and toddler teachers who are preparing to apply for the Child Development Associate (CDA) credential. One of my coaches, whom I'll call Rhonda, was struggling with a toddler teacher whom I'll call Vicki. At the time, we were offering both online and in-person CDA training, with both groups completing the required coursework during the same time frame. Vicki was completing the coursework online, but she had fallen behind on modules 3 and 4. Rhonda felt frustrated, believing that Vicki was uninterested in the program and not making progress. Vicki also felt frustrated and was thinking about dropping out of the program. The director of the child-care center where Rhonda and Vicki worked (whom I'll call Sheila) contacted me, and we set up a meeting for the four of us to discuss the situation.

During the meeting, Vicki shared that she struggled with formal education and was having a hard time with her online classes. Sheila offered to help her with the coursework. I recommended that Vicki start attending the in-person training (which Rhonda was teaching) starting with module 5 so that she didn't get any further behind. At the same time, she and Sheila could work on getting caught up on modules 3 and 4 online. Vicki was reluctant to attend the in-person sessions, but she finally agreed.

When Vicki first started coming to the in-person sessions, she did not participate much. I encouraged Rhonda to show excitement about Vicki's attendance and to give her lots of positive feedback. Rhonda did not think that it would make a difference, but she agreed to try it.

It took several months of these efforts, but an amazing transformation happened between Vicki and Rhonda. Because of Rhonda's consistent encouragement, Vicki began to believe that Rhonda cared about her. In turn, Vicki became more actively involved in improving her teaching practices. The two women went from disliking each other to becoming good friends. Vicki also started making connections with the other teachers attending the in-person sessions and began participating more often and joining in group discussions. She also completed the online modules with Sheila's help. Amazingly, Vicki was one of the first teachers in the group to receive her CDA credential. The key to this transformation? Relationship, relationship, relationship.

KEY PRACTICES FOR EFFECTIVE COACHING

A lot is expected of a coach, and these key practices make the journey more productive and enjoyable for everyone.

DIFFERENTIATING

Effective coaches recognize that each teacher is at a different level of understanding and proficiency. Furthermore, effective coaches respect how adults prefer to learn. For example, Chris just started his first teaching job and prefers to learn by reading information, Sequoia has been teaching for ten years and prefers to watch her coach model specific practices, and Ivy is a thirty-year veteran who prefers to watch a videotape of herself teaching. An effective coach individualizes what feedback she gives these teachers and how she provides it based on their needs, preferences, and abilities.

When effective coaches differentiate, they provide teachers with choices. They respect differences in how teachers approach and achieve desired outcomes. Effective coaches also focus on teachers' strengths, a practice that makes teachers more willing to change and enhance their teaching practices.

USING AUTHENTIC EXAMPLES

Teachers need authentic examples of what practices look like in early childhood classrooms. Your own experiences and examples from other classrooms work well for this purpose. You can also have teachers watch videos of themselves and of other teachers in action. Videos bring concepts to life and give visual images of teaching practices.

PROVIDING IMMEDIATE, SPECIFIC FEEDBACK

In a traditional teacher observation, a supervisor spends a short period watching and taking notes in a classroom while the teacher teaches. A few days or weeks later, the teacher and the supervisor meet to discuss the supervisor's findings. This method of giving feedback makes it hard for the teacher to remember what happened on the day of the observation, so she is less likely to understand the reasoning behind the coach's recommendations and make changes. On the other hand, when a teacher receives feedback shortly after a coaching observation, the observation-day experience is fresh in her mind, so she is better able to see the connections between what she did and what the coach suggests, is more receptive to the coach's suggestions, and is more likely to implement changes in a timely manner.

Specific feedback helps teachers see how their practices are relevant to the children they teach. Simply telling a teacher "good job" does not tell her what exactly she is doing well. In contrast, consider what a teacher learns when you say, "I noticed that you took time to find a magnifying glass and examine a bug with Rashad. You were sensitive to his interests and had a meaningful conversation about insects. Engaging in these types of interactions with children helps them feel connected and shows them that you value their interests."

Another way of involving teachers in giving themselves feedback is to ask each teacher to write herself a letter about what she plans on achieving during the next six months. The coach then keeps the letter. After six months, the coach returns the letter and asks the teacher to reflect on what she has accomplished since writing it. The teacher then determines the next steps in her PL journey. This strategy enables the teacher to receive specific feedback not only from her coach but also from herself, providing a chance for her to make deep and meaningful discoveries.

MODELING AND PRACTICING

When coaches observe teachers interacting with children in their classrooms, they gain understanding of the teachers' strengths and opportunities for growth. In turn, a teacher benefits from watching as her coach models how to implement specific strategies. Modeling provides a visual example of what to do and how to do it. Even more important is for the teacher to practice mirroring what her coach has modeled. This activity allows the coach to see whether the teacher correctly understands the technique and how to implement it. For example, a coach might model asking open-ended questions to the children in the teacher's classroom. Then, as the teacher asks open-ended questions, the coach observes and provides feedback.

Coaches and teachers sometimes feel uncomfortable modeling and practicing together. One coach, recognizing that a teacher felt uneasy about this activity, admitted her own discomfort and said she hoped that she and the teacher could have fun pretending together. This suggestion eased the teacher's tension, and they playfully practiced together. With time, most coaches and teachers become more comfortable with modeling and practicing.

CREATING PLANS OF ACTION AND REMINDERS

Do you ever create New Year's resolutions with great intentions? You may change your actions for a few days or even for several weeks or months, but then do your old habits start to creep back in? Have you ever woken up and thought, "Why am I not doing [insert resolution] anymore?" There is never one simple reason or explanation; generally, a number of factors are involved. The bottom line is that it takes time and energy to change, and the process is rarely easy.

I have discovered that I sustain new behaviors much more successfully if someone checks up on my progress. It also helps if this person encourages me to press forward and keep going. That is the power of coaching. Effective coaches provide encouragement, check on progress, and exact accountability.

To help in the process of sustaining change, teachers and coaches create plans of action together. A plan of action is a step-by-step guide for implementing new practices. To create these plans, coaches ask what teachers want to learn about and what is important to them. By discovering teachers' learning interests, coaches can help teachers set more-meaningful goals as part of their plans of action. The best plans of action contain goals that apply newly learned practices to daily teaching activities. It is not enough for teachers to cognitively understand teaching techniques; they need to know what these strategies will look and sound like in their own classrooms. (For more information about plans of action, see chapter 8.)

Once plans of action are established, coaches should remind teachers about their shared goals. These reminders could be notes, phone calls, emails, or text messages. A coach can even use an app such as Remind to send suggestions and encouragement to every teacher in her coaching cohort. These messages can be specific (such as, "Just a friendly reminder to remember to greet all the children in your class by name when they arrive each morning") or general (such as, "Remember to work on implementing your plan of action this week"). Coaches can also personalize their messages to individual teachers based on specific plans of action.

REFLECTIVE LISTENING

As any early childhood professional knows, working with young children can be exciting, frustrating, exhausting, and joyful—all in the same day! Add that to whatever feelings a teacher has about being coached, and you will see that helping teachers manage emotions is an important part of coaching.

To this end, one of a coach's key tools is reflective listening. Reflective listening requires the coach to listen with full attention, including making eye contact. She must focus on the teacher's message and seek clarification as needed. By providing feedback, the coach helps the teacher know that she is heard and understood. The coach must also pay attention to nonverbal cues—for example, a teacher might say one thing yet convey a very different message with her body language. In reflective listening, coaches hear out teachers' points of view and are open to differences of opinion. They pay attention to what they hear and the feelings attached to those messages.

Reflecting Emotions

One important tool of reflective listening is reflecting emotions. Even if teachers do not specifically state how they feel, their emotions show themselves through tone, volume, body language, and vocabulary. Coaches should reflect these emotions by naming them and their causes. For example:

- "It sounds like you're frustrated because . . ."
- "You seem disappointed that . . ."
- "It appears you're excited about . . ."

When a coach reflects emotions, the teacher can recognize and process them. This practice also validates the teacher's feelings and helps her feel understood.

Summarizing

Another reflective-listening technique is summarizing, or restating in a few words what the teacher has shared. For example:

- "I heard you say that you feel the children aren't making as much progress as you'd like and that you're wondering what to do differently. Is that correct?"
- "It seems you're pleased with the lesson but also concerned that a couple of the children didn't seem to understand the concepts you presented. Is that right?"

By consolidating the information shared, summarizing provides clarity and helps the coach find out if she is understanding what the teacher is saying. A concise description of a situation is easier to comprehend, which, in turn, makes it easier to determine what to do next.

Barriers to Reflective Listening

A few common barriers can interfere with reflective listening. A receiver may misunderstand the speaker's message, become distracted and lose interest in the conversation, jump to an incorrect conclusion, or overreact. This last barrier can be particularly problematic because reacting with strong emotions can damage relationships.

For example, imagine that a teacher you coach mentions that she is drilling children with flashcards to teach them their ABCs. You, however, think that this activity is developmentally inappropriate and should never be used in early childhood. Even if you are right, telling the teacher at that moment how you really feel about the practice is probably ill advised. We all have our triggers about certain practices; however, no one likes to be blindsided by sudden strong criticism, so this type of reaction will probably make the teacher defensive rather than convince her to change.

In this type of situation, coaches can modulate their responses by determining the purpose of the teacher's communication. Is the teacher seeking facts, stating thoughts or beliefs that differ from the coach's, or expressing strong emotions? These statements illustrate each purpose:

- **Seeking facts:** "My dual-language learners are way behind in learning to read, even though I use the same materials and strategies for all the children. I don't know what I'm doing wrong."

- **Stating differing thoughts or beliefs:** "I don't problem solve with young children because they are too young to solve their own problems."

- **Expressing strong emotions:** "I can't believe this! You said to try buddy reading, and now my reading time is out of control."

Using these examples, here are some ways that coaches can approach each type of communication:

- **Seeking facts:** This teacher needs assistance in acquiring information. The coach can help the teacher find information on effective strategies for teaching dual-language learners to read.

- **Stating differing thoughts or beliefs:** Sometimes what we say and what we mean are different. Upon further discussion, the coach may discover that this teacher actually does believe that children can problem solve but does not think that they have the language skills to verbally go through the problem-solving steps. When the coach and teacher have differing opinions, what the teacher says is not necessarily wrong. It behooves the coach to find out more about the teacher's thought process. It is a good idea for both parties to discuss the teacher's ideas in depth. If thoughts or beliefs still differ, sometimes it is best to agree to disagree. Often with time and open discussions, teachers and coaches find common ground and understanding.

- **Expressing strong emotions:** This teacher needs the coach to validate her emotions and then discuss her concerns with her. For instance, the coach might say, "You seem upset. You're concerned because your reading time seems to be out of your control. Tell me more about what's happening."

OVERCOMING COMMON CHALLENGES TO COACHING

Certain challenges frequently arise during coaching. Coaches can use these strategies to ensure a successful experience for both teachers and themselves.

TEACHER RESISTANCE

Coaches may encounter initial resistance from some of the teachers they coach. Sometimes the resistance is subtle—for instance, the coach may notice a teacher's stiff body language and lack of engagement during coaching conversations. In other cases, the resistance is overt. For instance, a teacher might tell the coach outright that she (the teacher) has no intention of doing anything differently. Either way, the coach should not take the resistance personally, as it probably has little to do with the coach. Instead, the coach should use this obstacle as an opportunity to learn more about the teacher and what she needs. Generally, as a relationship of trust develops between the coach and the teacher, resistance decreases. In rare instances where the resistance is extreme, coaches can discuss the matter with administrators and determine whether or not coaching should continue.

PERSONALITY CLASHES

Ideally, administrators can prevent conflicts by taking personalities into account when making coaching assignments. However, sometimes a teacher and a coach discover that they simply do not get along. If you find yourself in this situation, try these tips:

- Remember that each teacher is a unique individual with differing needs and interests.

- Relationship, relationship, relationship! Build your rapport with each teacher.

- Be empathetic. Focus and reflect on the teacher's point of view.

- Understand that collaborative partnerships take time. Meet each teacher where she is today.

Many personality clashes can be overcome if both parties look past their differences and focus on their shared, and most important, objective: enhancing the learning and development of young children. But in extreme cases, an administrator may need to reassign the teacher to a different coach.

SCHEDULING

Time constraints are often a challenge for a coach. Some of these difficulties come from the coach's responsibilities, such as having a large coaching load or other job demands that take time away from coaching. Coaching sessions may have to be canceled because of teacher absences or staff shortages that make it hard to find classroom coverage at the necessary time. Special events, such as parties or field days, can also affect the coaching schedule. Be flexible, persistent, and creative.

Coaching can be a powerful PL strategy for facilitating positive changes in teaching practices. Remember to focus on building strong and respectful relationships with teachers and creating trusting, reciprocal coaching partnerships.

CHAPTER 7:

Helping Teachers Become Reflective

Sarah, a preschool teacher, notices that several children in her classroom are struggling during circle time. They are wiggly and noisy and sometimes even get up and leave the circle. As she reflects on what to do, Sarah wonders if her circle time is too long or if she is not keeping the children's interest. She brainstorms ideas and discusses them with her coach. Eventually, Sarah decides to shorten her circle time and to provide the children with more props and movement activities during circle time. She also plans some alternative activities that children can do with her co-teacher if they need a break from circle time.

WHAT IS REFLECTION?

To reflect means to thoughtfully ponder or contemplate actions, events, and concepts. Donald Schon lists two types of reflection in his book *The Reflective Practitioner: How Professionals Think in Action:*

- *Reflection-**in**-action* refers to reflecting on an event as it takes place. For example, as a teacher reads a book to his class during circle time, he notices that the children are restless. He thinks about his own actions and the children's and decides to engage the children in a movement activity.

- *Reflection-**on**-action* refers to reflecting on an event after it has taken place. This type of reflection happens, for example, when a teacher thinks about events that happened earlier in the day and considers what went well and what he could do differently in the future.

Coaches guide teachers to both types of reflection. Each type helps teachers become more aware of how their choices affect children's learning and development.

BENEFITS OF REFLECTION

Reflection enables teachers to link their knowledge to their practices. Sometimes a disconnect exists between what teachers *know* are best practices and what teachers actually *do*. For example, I once coached an experienced teacher on guidance techniques within an inclusive classroom. As the teacher and I reflected on her practice, she shared that she knew she should be implementing certain strategies in her classroom, but she had become lax and stopped engaging in those practices. She committed to renew her efforts in this area. As this experience shows, reflection during coaching gives teachers opportunities to think deeply about whether their actions align with their knowledge and understanding.

REFLECTION TECHNIQUES

Reflection can take many forms. Here are some useful ones.

REPLAYING

This exercise helps the teacher and the coach reflect on past experiences and test other ways to handle similar situations. A teacher can complete this activity individually, or the coach can guide the teacher through it and discuss the questions with him:

1. Quiet your mind.

2. Mentally replay the experience. Think objectively about your actions. What did you do? What effect did it have?

3. Rewind the scene, and imagine it again. This time, picture yourself using an alternative strategy, and let the situation play out.

4. Think about what happened in the new version of the experience. How was your behavior different? How did the children react to it?

5. Repeat these steps with different ideas until you feel comfortable with one.

6. Write out your idea and create a plan of action for how you will implement the idea.

ASKING NONJUDGMENTAL QUESTIONS

This tool helps a coach to both build trust with and make suggestions to a teacher. If the teacher mentions taking an action that had negative consequences, the coach's first instinct may be to ask, "Why did you do that?" However, this type of question often comes across as critical and may cause the teacher to become defensive. Instead, the coach could ask, "What could you do differently next time?" This type of question leads the teacher to think more deeply about the situation and to formulate alternative strategies. It also shows that the coaching partnership is a safe environment in which the teacher can discuss his ideas, perceptions, actions, and feelings with a supportive listener.

JOURNALING

Journaling helps teachers intentionally reflect on actions, knowledge, and practices. Writing down your thoughts can add clarity to your ideas. Write about what you tried and how it worked (or did not work). Write about what you are learning. Write about what you have observed about the children in your classroom: How did they respond to your actions? What did they say or do? Writing down your thoughts often gives you new insights about a situation. The act of writing can help you solve problems because it enables you to consider different solutions.

As you start journaling, it may help to use prompts such as these:

• The best thing that happened today was . . .

• The children responded positively when I . . .

• Today I learned . . .

• I had a positive impact when I . .

Journal regularly, and go back and reread previous entries. Be reflective. You may be surprised by just how much you have grown and developed!

REFLECTIVE INQUIRY AND PERSPECTIVE TAKING

Reflective inquiry involves asking thought-provoking questions to lead to new understanding. Reflective inquiry is often a future-oriented approach, asking, "What would happen if I . . . ?" It requires teachers to more closely examine their current practices and possible changes to them.

One way to engage in reflective inquiry is through perspective taking, or looking at a situation from another viewpoint. Each person has different biases, values, and beliefs, and individuals tend to view experiences through their personal lenses. When a teacher takes other perspectives, he begins to see new possibilities.

There are two types of perspective taking. One uses the viewpoint of an individual (people perspective taking), and the other focuses on aspects of the environment (environmental perspective taking). Let's look at each type.

People Perspective Taking

People perspective taking requires looking at a classroom situation through the perspective of another person, such as a child or a coach. The teacher asks himself questions such as, "How would a child view this incident?" or "What might my coach think about my interactions with the children?" People perspective taking opens the teacher's mind to how others might feel and how they might view the situation differently. This understanding leads to new insights and can influence the teacher's future responses and actions.

People perspective taking works particularly well when teachers face challenging behaviors in their classrooms. Most teachers would love for coaches to identify one cause and one solution to these kinds of difficulties, but typically, many variables affect children's actions. Instead of simply trying to fix the behavior, teachers and coaches need to step back and get a complete view of the scenario. To start, the coach might have the teacher ask himself the following questions:

• What is the child communicating with this behavior?

• What am I communicating with my behavior?

• Am I being consistent, or am I sending contradictory messages (such as speaking hurtful words while smiling and using a kind tone)?

The answers to these questions can provide surprising details that will help the teacher and the coach decide how to address the issue. For example, I used people perspective taking while helping a preschool teacher whom I'll call Garissa. She stated that one of the children in her classroom, whom I'll call Mateo, constantly had behavior issues, such as pushing and hitting other children. I agreed to observe the classroom to gather more information.

During the observation, I saw that Mateo was a busy child who frequently touched something or someone. Interestingly, he had no negative interactions or behaviors during the forty-five minutes in which he ate lunch and engaged in a hands-on activity. I also noticed that the classroom had few sensory activities available for the children and that transitions between activities took a long time. For instance, it took over fifteen minutes for Garissa to set up the cots for nap time. During these intervals, many of the children engaged in disruptive behavior. However, Garissa seemed unaware of how long it took her to complete tasks. She was also easily distracted from those tasks by children needing her attention and was generally more reactive then proactive.

After the observation, I thought about the situation from Mateo's perspective and then from Garissa's. The results gave me a wealth of information. I used my findings to create a plan that could help not just Garissa and Mateo but all the children in the class.

When I met with Garissa, I helped her engage in perspective taking from a child's point of view. She began to consider some of the reasons for the behavior that the children exhibited in her classroom. Maybe Mateo needed frequent sensory feedback and was getting it the only way he knew how: by touching people and objects constantly. Perhaps when Garissa was involved in a lengthy task and there were limited activities available, the children became bored and decided to create their own fun and games. These discoveries helped Garissa to recognize how her actions could be contributing to Mateo's and the other children's challenging behavior. She began brainstorming ways to change her own behavior.

Through intensive coaching, both Mateo and Garissa made positive changes in the classroom. Garissa added more sensory opportunities for the children and provided engaging activities during transitions. She also became more aware of when Mateo behaved appropriately and gave him positive feedback. As Mateo's needs were met, his challenging behaviors decreased.

Another way to help teachers use people perspective taking is to have them think about what their coaches would say. One teacher shared that she thinks about hearing her coach's voice in her head when she is teaching. This voice reminds the teacher of things she wants to do and say, helps her catch herself when she does something less effective, and makes her more aware of her actions in the moment. The coach's remembered words help the teacher make immediate course corrections even when the coach is not physically present.

Environmental Perspective Taking

Environmental perspective taking involves examining physical and emotional aspects of the classroom environment. The teacher and the coach reflect on a specific situation and ask themselves these types of questions:

- **Environment and room arrangement:** How do the environment and room arrangement influence this situation and these behaviors? If children are running in the classroom, is it because the environment includes tempting wide-open spaces? If the children are complaining that it is too noisy to read in the library area, is it because the room is arranged with the library area next to the dramatic-play area?

- **Schedule, routines, and transitions:** How do the classroom routines and transitions influence this situation and these behaviors? If children are falling asleep during lunch time, does your schedule need to be adjusted? If children are exhibiting challenging behaviors during transitions, is it because they are having to wait with nothing to do?

- **Learning experiences:** What types of learning experiences do we offer in the classroom, and how do the children receive them? What role do the learning experiences have in this situation? If children are not interested in participating in a learning experience, is it because the experience is too easy or too hard? If given a choice, where do children naturally go? What types of learning experiences interest the children and hold their attention?

- **Emotional climate and human interactions:** What is the emotional climate of the room? How would you describe the interactions between teachers and children? How might the emotional climate and interactions between children and teachers affect the situation? When children feel connected to teachers, are there fewer instances of challenging behavior? How would you feel if you were a child who spent eight to ten hours per day in your classroom?

- **Outside factors:** What outside factors could influence this situation? Does something in the program's structure or climate contribute to the issue? For example, if the teacher does not feel safe, secure, and valued within his position, he may struggle to help the children feel safe, supported, and valued.

As useful as environmental perspective taking is, sometimes the teacher and even the coach are too close to the classroom situation to effectively analyze it. In this case, they might ask another person with expertise on early childhood environments to conduct some environmental perspective taking in the classroom and write up his findings. Then the teacher and the coach can review the report, reflect on how the environment may affect children's behavior, and brainstorm strategies for addressing any concerns.

Sometimes an environmental perspective can reveal a surprisingly easy solution to a problem. For example, a toddler teacher whom I'll call Liz expressed frustration because the children in her classroom had a hard time staying in their chairs during snack and lunch, an issue that caused frequent disruptions. Using environmental perspective taking, Liz looked more closely at her classroom, specifically at the tables and chairs. She was surprised to discover that these items were actually too large for the children. Their feet dangled down and did not touch the ground, making it difficult for them to maintain stability as they ate. The children were not intentionally misbehaving—they were simply losing their balance and falling out of their chairs! Fortunately, Liz's child-care center received funding to purchase new tables and chairs, and Liz was amazed at the difference they made. With appropriately sized furniture, the children now stayed in their seats during snack and lunch.

REFLECTION FOR COACHES

Reflection is just as important for coaches as it is for teachers, especially since coaches educate teachers about reflecting. Along with helping teachers learn the strategies in this chapter, coaches should regularly reflect on their own perceptions and then expand their viewpoints to begin to see early childhood experiences through new eyes.

If you are a coach, think about the last time you walked into an early childhood classroom. What drew your attention: the environment, the routines, the learning experiences, or the emotional climate? What did you think and feel about what you observed? Were you able to be objective? Did you use people or environmental perspective taking? The answers to these questions can reveal your own next steps.

As a coach, it is important to reflect on your interactions with the teachers you coach. Do you make a positive connection with each teacher? How does each teacher react to your visits? Is he happy to meet with you, or does he seem annoyed and anxious to return to his classroom? Are you noticing any changes in his practices? Is he actively implementing the plans of action that you create during coaching sessions? Does the teacher need more encouragement or opportunities to practice new skills? What actions might you take to be a more effective coach?

The act of self-reflection helps us be more mindful of our actions and the effects those actions have on others. As mentioned earlier, coaches need to practice what they preach and take time to be reflective.

A common next step for coaches is identifying and overcoming biases. In the early childhood field, coaches may have biases about different curriculum approaches or guidance techniques. For instance, you may favor a specific philosophy, such as Reggio Emilia, Montessori, or High Scope. You might feel strongly about the ways early childhood environments should look or be organized. These biases can influence your words and actions. Everyone has biases, often without even being aware of them. While these attitudes do not make a coach a bad person, they may cloud how he feels about what he sees and hears during observations and coaching conversations. Recognizing his own biases allows a coach to catch himself and strive to think objectively. One way to do this is to set aside your preferences (biases) and think about the impact of a practice on the children. How are they acting and reacting? Focusing on the children can help you have a more objective viewpoint.

A coach also benefits from fostering an open mind before each coaching session. Be inquisitive about why the teacher is doing what he is doing. Always enter a classroom curious to discover more about the teacher, the children, and the environment.

Because coaches help teachers in many challenging situations, coaches often encounter situations that push their buttons. Everyone has triggers. While coaches cannot always avoid encountering theirs, they can learn to identify them and control their reactions. To help in this process, coaches should ask themselves these questions:

- What behaviors and environments provoke an emotional response for you? For example, do you tense up when you see a messy classroom or feel angry when you hear a teacher talking to a child in a sarcastic tone?

- When you encounter a trigger, whom do you empathize with: the teacher, the child, or yourself? Your perspective can help you determine your next steps. If you empathize with yourself, for example, stop and consider the perspectives of the teacher and the children. Take time to think about the situation from all three perspectives.

- How can you calm yourself down and restore clear thinking after experiencing a trigger?

By recognizing and responding appropriately to their triggers, coaches can strive to be as objective as possible and can help teachers do the same.

CHAPTER 8:

Coaching with the Reflective Strengths-Based Coaching Model

Annalee, an experienced coach, is used to telling teachers everything they are doing wrong and what to do instead. She loves being the expert and sharing her knowledge. She knows that some teachers dislike having her as a coach, but they really need her help!

At Annalee's new job, however, she is learning to use the RSBC Model. This model requires coaches to function as partners with teachers rather than experts: focusing on teachers' strengths, creating shared goals and plans of action, and modeling and practicing strategies together. Though Annalee is skeptical of this method at first, after three months, she finds that her coaching sessions have become much more productive. She has developed meaningful relationships with the teachers she coaches and has seen improvements in their practices. Now the teachers actually look forward to having Annalee coach them.

WHAT IS THE RSBC MODEL?

The Reflective Strengths-Based Coaching (RSBC) Model is a positive, encouraging, and affirming coaching system. This type of coaching identifies and builds on teachers' strengths—what teachers are doing well, rather than what they are doing wrong—to promote teachers' learning and create positive changes in practice. RSBC is built on the type of partnership described in chapter 6: a coach and a teacher working together in a positive, collaborative relationship to enhance the teacher's attitudes, skills, and knowledge so she can implement best practices for young children and their families.

So what is the difference between the coaching processes described in chapter 6 and the RSBC Model? The RSBC Model uses the processes from chapter 6 but takes them a step further by organizing them into a specific format, including a process called RSBC Conversations. These teacher-coach interactions take place after the coach has observed the teacher within the classroom environment. Using a step-by-step outline to structure the conversation, the coach honors the teacher's strengths, promotes reflection, and expands learning.

It can be stressful for a teacher to have someone observe her teaching, especially if she believes the observer is looking only for what the teacher is doing wrong. But in RSBC, teachers learn to relax, because they know that their coaches look for the positive things happening in their classrooms. Furthermore, RSBC promotes self-awareness. Teachers can focus on what they are doing well—and, perhaps counterintuitively, they also learn to better recognize opportunities for growth.

INFLUENCES FOR THE RSBC MODEL

I developed the RSBC Model over time with the help of several important influences. One was the excellent book *Coaching with Powerful Interactions* by Judy Jablon, Amy Dombro, and Shaun Johnsen. These authors emphasize a strengths-based coaching perspective and outline three main steps for coaching: be present, connect, and extend learning. They suggest having coaches conduct a "Me Check" to determine whether they are prepared and emotionally ready before each coaching session. They also recommend that coaches notice teachers' moments of effectiveness and use "I noticed" statements to share strengths-based feedback.

Another influence on the RSBC Model was a system presented during a training session I attended on intensive coaching, a special program hosted by TNTP (the New Teacher Project) in the state of Nevada. This system included strong modeling and practicing components. Additionally, one of the trainers used the terms *glows* for strengths and *grows* for opportunities for improvement, both of which I included in the RSBC Model.

The third major influence on the RSBC Model was the concept of reflective inquiry, including giving teachers multiple opportunities for reflection during coaching conversations. When teachers have time to reflect during coaching, they find the answers to problems within themselves. This approach is much more powerful than relying on coaches (or anyone else) to provide solutions. In the RSBC Model, teachers look at their teaching practices through different lenses and think about what they know and how they can use that knowledge to inform what they do and say.

WHY USE THE RSBC MODEL?

One benefit of using the RSBC Model is that it is particularly helpful for new coaches, as it clearly outlines the types of things to say and do during a coaching conversation. Coaches can use the RSBC Conversation Planning Sheet in appendix G to outline the key components of conversations before meeting with teachers. This sheet also gives coaches a guide to follow during meetings. Even seasoned coaches have stated that following the RSBC Model has helped them have more-productive coaching conversations.

For some coaches, especially experienced ones who have established a comfortable format for coaching, the RSBC Conversation may feel too structured. Remember, there is some flexibility in the implementation and order of the steps. If the coach forgets to ask whether the teacher has any questions, for example, the coach can easily follow up with a text or an email. If time is too limited to complete all the steps, the coach should select the steps that she feels are the most essential. However, I highly encourage coaches to not eliminate the modeling and practicing sections, as these steps greatly increase the chances of teachers' successfully implementing new strategies. This is especially true if coaches set a specific time frame for teachers to report on their progress.

One of my coaches, whom I'll call Emory, demonstrated how a coach can appropriately adapt the steps of the RSBC Model to meet a teacher's specific needs. On this particular day, I was observing as Emory coached a toddler teacher, whom I'll call Isabella. Partway through the conversation, Isabella shared a pressing concern. A child in Isabella's classroom had recently lost her father, and Isabella wanted to help this child and her family but did not know how. Emory recognized this important, immediate need and responded with flexibility and sensitivity. Rather than deferring the issue until its designated step in the discussion, she gave Isabella time to share her thoughts and feelings and provided emotional support. Then Emory shared some strategies that Isabella could try and promised to send Isabella some additional resources about loss and grief. With this concern now addressed, Emory and Isabella continued with the rest of the planned conversation. When Emory returned to her office, she immediately found several appropriate resources and sent them to Isabella, who thanked Emory for her quick response and support during a difficult situation.

RSBC CONVERSATIONS

RSBC Conversations include twenty-six steps. Don't worry—that number is not as overwhelming as it sounds! The steps are split into four main sections (the Four Cs):

- C1: Create Caring Connections
- C2: Communicate Shared Goals
- C3: Construct and Expand Learning
- C4: Closing Connections

Each of the Four Cs has two parts, and each part includes specific steps. Each step is summarized with a key word or phrase that helps you follow the model.

Let's now examine this model in detail. Each step includes a recommended time frame to keep the coaching conversation to around thirty minutes. If you want to have a longer or shorter discussion, adjust the times in each section to fit your needs.

C1: CREATE CARING CONNECTIONS (THREE TO FIVE MINUTES)

C1 builds positive connections within the coaching partnership as you highlight the teacher's strengths, affirm and validate her actions, and encourage her to continue the best practices she is already using.

Part 1	Part 2
Greet	Outline
Thank	Talk (Teacher)
Connect	Affirm

Part 1: Greet, Thank, and Connect

In C1, Part 1, you create a strong, healthy connection with the teacher.

Greet

Start with a genuine, enthusiastic greeting that includes calling the teacher by name.

> COACH: Nicki, it's really great to see you today!

Thank

Thank the teacher for allowing you to observe and for being willing to participate in a coaching session.

> COACH: Thank you so much for letting me observe your classroom today and for meeting with me.

Connect

Ask a connecting question related to the teacher's life.

> COACH: How are you doing today? How's your son doing?

These types of connecting questions help you learn more about the teacher and demonstrate interest in her as a person. However, you may find that some connecting questions can hijack the conversation. For example, if asking a teacher about her children will lead to a lengthy description of her son's latest soccer game, you might want to ask a different type of connecting question.

Part 2: Outline, Talk (Teacher), and Affirm

In C1, Part 2, you begin the coaching part of the conversation by explaining the agenda and discussing the observation with the teacher.

Outline

Give a brief overview that outlines how the conversation will proceed. Make each overview unique by outlining the specific items you will cover that day.

> COACH: Today, we'll start by having you share what went well in the dramatic-play center during my observation. Then we'll discuss your goal from our last coaching session about using complex vocabulary with the children. We'll set a new goal related to helping children develop reasoning skills, and we'll create a plan of action for meeting the goal. I'll model some strategies, and you'll have an opportunity to practice them. Then we'll reflect on those practices and determine next steps. Does that sound okay to you?

This step establishes the expectations for the conversation. If the discussion starts to go off track, the outline provides a mechanism for returning to the agreed-upon focus. It is important that coaching conversations do not become venting or feel-good sessions that do not contain any substance. Remember, your role is both to support the teacher and to keep the conversation on topic. Validate the teacher's feelings, listen respectfully to her concerns, encourage her to address them with the appropriate people, and then gently remind her of the agreed-upon topics. Helpful phrases include, "Let's go back to the topic of language modeling" (or whatever the focus is) and "I'd love to hear more about that after we finish our coaching conversation, if there's time."

For example, if a teacher is upset and starts to vent, a coach could say, "I can tell that you're upset about some of the things that are happening at your program. I understand your frustration. When we're done here, I think you should talk to your supervisor about your concerns. Right now, we need to focus on what you can do for the children in your classroom. Today I noticed that you'd added some interesting new materials to the math center. Tell me more about them." In this example, the coach validates the teacher's feelings, directs her to the appropriate source for discussing her concerns, and steers the coaching conversation back on track.

Talk (Teacher)

Teachers need opportunities to reflect and talk during coaching conversations. After giving the outline for the conversation, ask the teacher to reflect on the observation and then share what she thought went well. In other words, you are having the teacher give herself strengths-based feedback. To help the teacher remember specific experiences, remind her of where she was, what she was doing, and with whom she was interacting. For example, you might say something like this: "Let's talk about what happened while you were building a fort with Michael and Rachel in the block area." Give the teacher a few moments to reflect on the experience before asking her to share her thoughts and insights.

> COACH: Take a few minutes to think about what you were doing in the dramatic-play area with Amy and Tyrone. Tell me about that experience. What do you think went well?
>
> TEACHER: (*Takes time to think before responding.*) Amy and Tyrone seemed really excited about the flower-shop props I'd added to the center. They were sorting the flowers by color and creating signs listing how much each type of flower cost. There was a lot of conversation. I enjoyed playing along, being a customer, and buying flowers.

Affirm

After the teacher shares her feedback on the experience, affirm that feedback, paraphrase her response, and give positive "I noticed" statements based on the observation.

> COACH: I agree. Amy and Tyrone were very engaged in running the flower shop and enjoyed having you as a customer. I noticed that you were asking open-ended questions, such as, "What do you think we could do with the flowers?" Those questions expanded the conversation and prompted the children to think more deeply about what they were doing and how they could expand their play.

C2: COMMUNICATE SHARED GOALS (FIVE TO SEVEN MINUTES)

In C2, you collaborate with the teacher to determine goals that you both agree to work on together.

Part 1	Part 2
Follow Up	Introduce
Learning	Reflect (Teacher)
Expand	New Goal

Part 1: Follow Up, Learning, and Expand

In C2, Part 1, you and the teacher examine the results of the last coaching session and consider ways to expand the children's learning and engagement.

Follow Up

Discuss with the teacher the shared goal, plan of action, and reflection from the previous coaching session.

COACH: At our last coaching session, we set a shared goal to use complex vocabulary while the children are engaged in activities, and we created an action plan. Share with me—what's happened since we last met?

TEACHER: I've been trying to add complex vocabulary when I talk to the children about what they're doing. When we were setting up the flower shop, I told them the different names of the flowers, such as *carnation, daffodil,* and *chrysanthemum.* We talked about using the *cash register* and *making change* after someone buys some flowers.

COACH: Good to hear. I like how you're expanding the children's vocabulary by adding the flower-shop props to your dramatic-play area. Here's some of the complex vocabulary I heard you use today: *calculating the cost of the flowers* and *designing a beautiful bouquet.*

Learning

Ask the teacher questions that link the children's learning and engagement to the shared goal. Here are some useful questions to ask during this step:

- "Did implementing [the strategy from the last shared goal] affect children's learning and engagement?"

- "If not, why not?"

- "If yes, what was the effect?"

COACH: What did you notice about Amy's and Tyrone's engagement when you used complex vocabulary? What do you think they were learning when you added those words to the conversation?

TEACHER: I noticed that Amy and Tyrone were paying attention to what I was saying. They've been learning and using new words. Amy asked me which flower was the chrysanthemum. Tyrone wanted me to look at his bouquet. I loved hearing them use the new vocabulary.

Expand

Ask the teacher to share ideas for continuing to expand the children's learning and engagement. Share additional ideas for her consideration.

> COACH: How could you continue to expand the children's learning and engagement to help them develop their vocabularies?
>
> TEACHER: I plan on changing the dramatic-play area to a new theme every month. I was thinking we could have a veterinarian clinic and talk about taking care of different kinds of pets.
>
> COACH: That sounds like a great idea. You might want to ask the children for ideas for themes. You could also expand their vocabularies by reading books about topics related to the themes you use. Take time to define the new words as you read, and then find opportunities to use the words throughout the day. Encourage the children to use the words in their conversations with you.

Part 2: Introduce, Reflect (Teacher), and New Goal

During C2, Part 2, you move on to a new area of focus for coaching, give the teacher time to reflect on her current practices, and work with the teacher to determine a new shared goal. (Note: Even though you will be helping the teacher create a new goal in this part of the conversation, continue to support her efforts to achieve her previous goals, and look for ways to reinforce the continual implementation of these practices.)

Introduce

Introduce and define the new area of focus, such as supporting children's language development. It helps if you have identified a new focus area ahead of time. However, the teacher could also choose the new area of focus.

> COACH: Our next area of focus for coaching is helping the children develop their reasoning and thinking skills. We use reasoning skills to predict future events, solve problems, and find cause-and-effect relationships. You can use "why" and "how" questions to stimulate the children's thinking and to give them opportunities to explain their thinking processes.

Reflect (Teacher)

Have the teacher reflect on and share how her current practices relate to the new focus area. If classroom- and child-assessment data are available, they can give a clearer picture of what is actually happening in the classroom. For example, you and the teacher could examine child-outcome data and then reflect on the areas in which the children are thriving and the areas in which they need additional support.

COACH: Let's reflect on your current practices. What are you currently doing to help the children in your room develop their reasoning skills?

TEACHER: I ask the children questions about what they're doing, and I have them help solve classroom problems, such as what to do if too many children want to play with the same toy. Last week, when too many children wanted to ride the tricycles at the same time, I asked the children how we could solve the problem. The children figured out a tricycle-riding schedule that has been working really well.

COACH: That's great. Giving children opportunities to problem solve helps them develop their reasoning skills. Another opportunity for growth could be to ask the children more open-ended questions that start with *how* or *why*. You could also use your math and science materials in new ways to stimulate reasoning skills.

New Goal

Discuss with the teacher opportunities for growth, and cooperatively determine a new shared goal. This goal has two parts:

1. The desired outcome

2. The strategy that the teacher will implement with the coach's support to achieve that outcome

The desired outcome often involves helping children build a particular skill.

COACH: How do you think you could help the children in your classroom develop their reasoning skills?

TEACHER: I could have them do some science experiments so we could talk about cause and effect. Or I could have them make some predictions.

COACH: Yes, both of those are good ideas. Which ones do you think would be the most beneficial?

TEACHER: I like the idea of asking questions and having the children make predictions.

COACH: Okay. Let's start the new goal with the phrase "To develop children's reasoning skills by . . ." You complete the rest.

TEACHER: How about "To develop children's reasoning skills by asking 'how' and 'why' questions and having children make predictions"?

COACH: Great. Would you like me to send you an article on this topic that includes some implementation ideas?

TEACHER: Yes, that would be helpful.

Regardless of who chooses the new focus area, have the teacher determine the specific goal within that area based on her interests and needs. In the example conversation, the new shared goal breaks down as follows:

- **Desired outcome:** To develop children's reasoning skills

- **Strategy (what the teacher does to achieve that outcome):** Asking "how" and "why" questions and having children make predictions

C3: CONSTRUCT AND EXPAND LEARNING (FIFTEEN TO TWENTY MINUTES)

This component is the core reason for you and the teacher to meet and plan together, so it should take up the majority of the coaching-conversation time. During this component, you and the teacher create a plan of action based on the new shared goal.

Part 1	Part 2
Plan	Model How
Define What	Practice Now
Explain Why	Reflect (Teacher)
Identify When, Where, and with Whom	Set Check-In Date

Part 1: Plan, Define What, Explain Why, and Identify When, Where, and with Whom

During C3, Part 1, you and the teacher create a plan of action that details how you will both work toward the shared goal.

Plan

Have the teacher start writing down ideas for the plan of action.

> COACH: Okay, we have our shared goal: "To develop children's reasoning skills by asking 'how' and 'why' questions and having children make predictions." Now we need to create a plan of action to achieve that goal. First, get out a "Plan of Action Geometric Form" and write down the goal.

Creating a plan of action provides several benefits. First, it gives the teacher an opportunity to write down ideas in her own words. This process gives her ownership in the plan. Second, the plan of action creates a structured guide for meeting the goal by listing and detailing a series of achievable steps.

There are many different worksheets or forms that you can use to create plans of action. Appendix H contains an example: the "Plan of Action Geometric Form," which uses geometric shapes to distinguish types of information. Regardless of what format you choose, you and the teacher both need copies of the completed plan of action. You can easily accomplish this by having the teacher fill out the form, taking a picture of it with your smartphone or other device, and having the teacher keep the hard copy.

Define What

Check the teacher's understanding of the shared goal by having her define the desired outcome and the strategy.

> COACH: We're focusing on developing reasoning skills. Tell me what that means to you.
>
> TEACHER: It's helping the children build their thinking skills—having them explain what they're thinking, such as by asking them, "How are you going to build a tall tower?"
>
> COACH: Good example. Write that definition of reasoning skills in the "What" section on your plan of action. One of the ways you wanted to promote those skills was to have the children make predictions. What does it mean to make a prediction?
>
> TEACHER: To guess what you think will happen.
>
> COACH: Yes. Write that definition in the "What" section, too. You can have the children predict what they think will happen next in a story and then ask them why they think that'll happen or how they know it'll happen. You can encourage the children to listen for hints and look for clues in the pictures as you're reading the story. The children could predict what they think they'll be having for lunch or predict how many blocks would fit into a box.

Explain Why

Have the teacher explain why the desired outcome is important for young children's growth and development.

> COACH: Why is it important for children to develop reasoning skills?
>
> TEACHER: It helps them think about things and learn about the world.

COACH: Yes, critical thinking and reasoning skills are essential for life and are important for school readiness. These skills help children learn how to make sound decisions and solve problems. We also build our brains by using our brains, so children build reasoning skills by using reasoning skills. Go ahead and put those reasons in the "Why" section on your plan of action.

Identify When, Where, and with Whom

Have the teacher flesh out the strategy by identifying when, where, and with whom she will teach the skill from the desired outcome.

COACH: Let's start thinking about what it'll look like when you ask the children to make predictions. When will you do it? Where in the room will it be happening? Which children will you do it with? How will you do it?

TEACHER: I thought it'd be fun to have the children predict what's inside a pumpkin. I could bring a pumpkin to school on Friday and have small groups of children give me their predictions during free-choice time. I could write the ideas on a chart in the science area.

COACH: Sounds like a great idea. Write all that down on your action plan.

TEACHER: (*Writing.*) Okay. So "With Whom" is "all the children." "When" is "Friday during free-choice time." And "Where" is "science area."

Part 2: Model How, Practice Now, Reflect (Teacher), and Set Check-In Date

During C3, Part 2, you help the teacher become comfortable using the strategy, understand its importance, and set up an accountability step.

Model How

Demonstrate the strategy to help the teacher visualize best practices. You can also expand the teacher's learning by providing other examples of the strategy, such as a video of someone using it.

Modeling can take place during the coaching session, but it does not have to. If it would be more effective for you to model the strategy in the teacher's classroom with the children, you and the teacher should determine an appropriate time for you to do so. In this example, the coach models the strategy during the coaching session.

COACH: I'm going to model one way to help children make predictions. I'll also model asking "why" questions. Let's pretend I'm the teacher and you're a child in my classroom. I want you to say and do things that the children in your classroom might say and do. Now, let's pretend it's free-choice time, and you're playing at the water table. I bring over a pinecone and say, "It looks like you're having fun. I was wondering if this pinecone will float or sink in the water. Would you like to make a *prediction*, or a good guess, and *predict* whether the pinecone will sink or float?"

TEACHER: (*Pretending to be a child.*) I think it'll sink.

COACH: So you *predict* the pinecone will sink. Why do you think it'll sink?

TEACHER: (*As a child.*) Because it's heavy and prickly.

COACH: Let's test your *prediction* and see what happens. Here's the pinecone. You can put it in the water. Did it sink or float?

TEACHER: (*As a child.*) It floated.

COACH: Why do you think it floated?

TEACHER: (*As a child.*) It wasn't heavy enough.

COACH: Good thinking! Would you like to find some other items and *predict* whether they'll sink or float?

TEACHER: (*As a child.*) Yes!

COACH: Thank you for role-playing with me. What did you notice while we did that?

TEACHER: I noticed that you defined the word *prediction* as "a good guess." You also used the words *predict* and *prediction* several times and followed up on my prediction by asking several "why" questions.

COACH: Yes. I'm glad you noticed those strategies. I also asked you if you wanted to continue the activity by finding other items for the water table. Any questions?

Practice Now

Actively trying a strategy is more powerful than merely seeing and hearing about it. Therefore, at this point, give the teacher an opportunity to practice the chosen strategy. This critical step gives the teacher time in a safe environment to gain the confidence and ability to implement the strategy effectively. Practicing also allows you to check for understanding, clarify, and give feedback.

COACH: I want you to practice what you plan to say to the children during your pumpkin-prediction activity. We were talking about your student Rachel earlier, so I'll pretend to be her.

TEACHER: Okay. Rachel, I want you to *predict*, or guess, what's inside the pumpkin.

COACH: (*Pretending to be Rachel.*) Candy. Can I have some?

TEACHER: Right now we're just guessing what's in the pumpkin. Later, we'll cut it open and see what's there. Why did you guess candy?

COACH: (*As Rachel.*) I like candy, and people give me candy when I go to houses that have pumpkins.

TEACHER: That's good thinking. So the pumpkin reminds you of a time when you received candy.

COACH: Okay, let's stop there. I really liked how you kept the conversation going and helped Rachel make the connection between pumpkins and candy. I was wondering if you might want to add some more explanation about the activity before you ask the children to make predictions. What do you think?

TEACHER: Yes, that'd be a good idea. I think I'll introduce the pumpkin during circle time and talk about making predictions, or good guesses. I'll let the children know that they can tell me their predictions in the science center during free-choice time.

COACH: That sounds like a good plan. Go ahead and list the specific steps you'll follow and the materials you'll need in the "How" section on your plan of action.

If you have longer coaching sessions, engage the teacher in additional modeling and practicing.

For instance, if more time had been available in our example, the coach could have modeled and had the teacher practice asking "how" and "why" questions. The coach and the teacher could then have brainstormed and created a list of opportunities for the teacher to ask these types of questions.

Reflect (Teacher)

Ask the teacher to reflect on how implementing the strategy will make a difference in children's lives. This reflection helps solidify the importance of the strategy in the teacher's mind, and it also reinforces the concept that the teacher's actions do make a difference.

COACH: Before we move on, I want you to take a few minutes to reflect. How will using "how" and "why" questions and asking the children to make predictions make a difference in their lives? You can share when you're ready.

TEACHER: (*Takes time to think before responding.*) I think it'll help the children be curious and develop their thinking skills. It should also help them be more interested in the pumpkin-prediction activity, and they'll want to find out what's really inside the pumpkin. It'll be fun for them to make predictions and see if their predictions are correct. It'll be interesting to see how many of the children already know what's inside a pumpkin. I hope the ones who don't know won't be too disappointed when they find out there are only pumpkin seeds and goop inside!

Set Check-In Date

With the teacher, determine a specific date by which she will complete and report on the plan of action and its outcomes.

> COACH: Let's set a check-in date. Since you're planning to do the pumpkin-prediction activity on Friday, when would you like to report?
>
> TEACHER: I'll text you on Friday afternoon and let you know how it went.
>
> COACH: That'd be great. It'd also be fun if you sent me a picture of your chart with all the predictions. Then we'll discuss the activity in more depth at our next coaching session.

Having a check-in date promotes accountability for taking action. If the teacher does not report back in a timely manner, reach out to her. In my experience, teachers are more likely to implement their plans of action when they set check-in dates with their coaches and their coaches follow up with them.

On the actual check-in day, listen to the teacher's report, express enthusiasm about the actions she has taken, and give her positive feedback. If the teacher explains that the implementation did not go as planned or has not happened yet, offer encouragement and set another check-in date.

C4: CLOSING CONNECTIONS (TWO TO THREE MINUTES)

In this final section, you thank the teacher for her efforts, encourage her to continue them, and explain the details of the next coaching session.

Part 1	Part 2
Thank	Questions
Encourage	Focus
Reflect (Teacher)	Next

Part 1: Thank, Encourage, and Reflect (Teacher)

C4, Part 1 reinforces positive connections between you and the teacher and encourages the teacher to keep reflecting.

Thank

Thank the teacher for her time, attention, and efforts.

> COACH: Thank you for letting me come observe your classroom and for meeting with me today. I really appreciated your attention and efforts in creating the plan of action and role playing together.

Encourage

Express excitement and encouragement about the agreed-upon next steps.

> COACH: I'm excited to hear about your pumpkin-prediction activity and how it goes when you ask the children "how" and "why" questions.

Reflect (Teacher)

Encourage the teacher to continue to reflect on her teaching practices and to plan on sharing her reflections at the next coaching session.

> COACH: Please keep reflecting on your teaching practices and how they make a difference in the lives of the children. I want to hear your thoughts at our next coaching session.

Part 2: Questions, Focus, and Next

C4, Part 2 involves concluding any unresolved issues from the current coaching session and preparing for the next one.

Questions

Ask the teacher whether she has any questions or concerns. If she does, address them.

> COACH: Do you have any questions?
>
> TEACHER: Yes, I do. What should I do if the children don't want to predict what's inside the pumpkin?
>
> COACH: You should always give children a choice about whether they participate. Sometimes a child might not want to participate at first but may be willing to after seeing other children do it. Encourage everyone to make predictions, but don't force it. If you have some children who are reluctant, you could say, "You can make a prediction whenever you're ready."
>
> TEACHER: Okay, thanks.

Focus

Make a closing connection with the teacher, and share the focus of the next coaching observation.

> COACH: I hope you have a great week. At our next observation, I'll be listening to hear you ask "how" and "why" questions. I'll also be watching to see if you have the children make any predictions.

Next

Inform the teacher of the date and time of the next coaching session, according to the schedule you have set up with the program administrators.

> COACH: Our next coaching session will be on Tuesday. I'll start observing your classroom at 9:00 a.m., and we'll meet for a coaching conversation around 9:30 a.m. See you next week.

Ideally, both the coach and teacher leave the coaching conversation feeling positive about the interaction and clear about the next steps. If not, the coach should follow up with the teacher to strengthen the relationship and add clarity to the next steps.

TOOLS FOR USING THE RSBC MODEL

When I developed the RSBC Model, I also worked to create tools that would help coaches successfully use the program. Appendices G, I, and J contain these tools. The next several sections explain what the tools are and how to use them.

RSBC CONVERSATION PLANNING SHEET

The RSBC Conversation Planning Sheet appears in appendix G. This tool helps you prepare for coaching conversations ahead of time. It briefly outlines each of the twenty-six steps of RSBC and provides space near each step to write notes and questions for the teacher. Twenty-six steps are a lot to remember, but a well-filled-out Planning Sheet serves as a guide during coaching conversations.

RSBC CONVERSATION REFLECTION TOOL

The RSBC Conversation Reflection Tool (CRT) appears in appendix I. This tool has three purposes:

1. It reminds coaches of the steps to correctly implement the RSBC Model.

2. It helps coaches engage in self-reflection and become more aware of how they coach.

3. It provides a useful format for supervisors to take notes as they observe coaches coaching.

The CRT includes twenty-six questions that correspond with the twenty-six steps of the RSBC Model. Each question starts with the phrase, "Did I/the coach . . ." so that the tool can be used for both self-reflection and supervisor observation. The person filling out the sheet checks yes or no for each question, writes notes if desired, and lists some glows (strengths) and grows (opportunities for improvement).

If you are a coach, you can use the CRT to look more closely at what actually happens during your coaching conversations. For instance, one new coach discovered that she spent most of her time on C1: Creating Caring Connections. She realized that although she loved telling teachers about all the great things she saw happening in their classrooms, this emphasis did not lead to many changes in the teachers' practices. Another new coach noted that she did not feel comfortable with modeling strategies or helping teachers practice them, so she often skipped those steps in her coaching conversations. With some additional practice—along with watching other coaches model and practice with teachers—this coach gained confidence in implementing these important steps.

RSBC CONVERSATION KEY WORD CHART

The RSBC Conversation Key Word Chart appears in appendix J. It provides a quick reference to help you remember the steps of the RSBC Model during coaching conversations. (Some coaches prefer to use only the Planning Sheet instead.) Some coaches provide a copy of the Key Word Chart for teachers to follow along with during coaching conversations. This allows a teacher to remind the coach if the coach forgets any of the steps!

COACHING COACHES

If you supervise coaches, you can use the RSBC Model and its tools to provide PL for your coaches. The CRT works particularly well for this purpose. You fill out one copy while observing a coaching session, and the coach completes another copy after the session. Then you and the coach meet to discuss both sets of reflections. During these feedback sessions, you can model many of the practices from the RSBC Model:

1. Start by establishing a caring connection with the coach.

2. Ask the coach to reflect on her practices and to share what she thinks went well during the coaching session.

3. Discuss progress on any goals from previous meetings.

4. Look at each of the four sections of the coaching conversation. If the coach missed any steps, discuss with her why it happened and how she can implement those steps in the future.

5. Have the coach share her reflections on each of the four sections. Note that you may not need to share your feedback if the coach shares something similar or identical. Plus, it is more powerful when the coach engages in self-discovery.

6. Brainstorm additional strategies with the coach, and problem solve any concerns.

7. Thank the coach for her time and attention during the meeting.

SAMPLE COACHING CONVERSATION BETWEEN A SUPERVISOR AND A COACH

This extended example shows a coaching conversation between a supervisor and coach. It is based on an actual conversation I had with a new coach who was learning how to use the RSBC Model. What similarities do you notice between this conversation and the teacher-coach conversation? What differences do you see?

The Conversation

SUPERVISOR: Good afternoon, Petra. Thank you for allowing me to observe your coaching session with Willie this morning. I enjoyed seeing you coach. How's your week been?

COACH: It's been a good week, but it's been really busy.

SUPERVISOR: I'm glad you're having a good week. It's a busy time of the year. Today we're going to talk about each of the four components from your coaching conversation and share our reflections. We'll also discuss your strengths and opportunities for growth. Does that sound okay to you?

COACH: Yes, that sounds good.

SUPERVISOR: Great. How do you think your coaching session went today? Let's start by discussing C1: Create Caring Connections.

COACH: I think it went pretty well. When I did my self-reflection, I noticed that I didn't give an overview and outline the conversation. Do I need to do that every time if we always follow the same format?

SUPERVISOR: Good question. Why do you think it might be important to outline the conversation with the teacher?

COACH: I guess it helps the teacher know what we'll talk about, but it feels repetitive.

SUPERVISOR: You can make each overview unique by outlining the specific items you're going to cover that day. For example, you could say, "Today for our coaching session, I want you to first share your thoughts about the interactions you had with the children in the writing center during the observation. Second, we'll discuss your progress on the science goals that we developed at our last session, and finally, we'll create a new goal about enhancing children's social-emotional development. We'll do some practicing and create a plan of action for our goal. How does that sound to you?" If the teacher agrees to your overview, it'll help direct your conversation.

COACH: Oh, I see; you're giving a fairly specific outline of what we're going to cover. That makes more sense than just saying, "I'm going to share some positive feedback, and then we'll create a plan of action."

SUPERVISOR: Yes. By giving an overview and being specific, you set the stage for the conversation you want to have with the teacher. If the conversation starts to go off track, the outline helps you steer the conversation back. Any questions about that step?

COACH: No, I think I understand what to do.

SUPERVISOR: Let's practice. Think about your next coaching session with Willie. Then I want you to practice giving an overview for that session. You may write down a few notes if that'd be helpful.

COACH: Okay. How should I start it?

SUPERVISOR: You could say, "Today for our coaching session, we'll first . . ."

COACH: Right. "Today for our coaching session, we'll first have you tell me about how you've been promoting children's higher-level thinking skills in the block center. Then we'll create a plan of action for expanding the science activities in your classroom."

SUPERVISOR: You gave a great overview on several parts of the coaching conversation. What else could you add?

COACH: I need to remember to state that we'll discuss the progress on the goals from the last session and that we'll be practicing strategies.

SUPERVISOR: Yes, that's important because it promotes accountability. Is there anything else you noticed from today's C1?

COACH: I didn't ask Willie to reflect and give feedback on what she thought went well during the observation.

SUPERVISOR: Yes. Why do you think that would be important to do during a coaching conversation?

COACH: If a teacher tells me what she thinks went well during the observation, I'll have a better idea about what she's thinking. Then I can add my positive feedback to what she said and intentionally point out things that she might not realize she's doing well.

SUPERVISOR: Yes, I noticed that you were very positive and enthusiastic with Willie and shared lots of positive feedback. But there's also power in sharing one simple statement and then pausing and letting it sink in. How do you feel when I say, "Thank you for your thoughtful self-reflection"? (Pause.)

COACH: I like that. I see what you mean. I always have so many good things I want to share; I sometimes get carried away.

SUPERVISOR: Can you think of some other ways to share your positive feedback? Maybe in writing?

COACH: I could put it in an email or text or—I know, I could even write a note and leave it with the teacher before I go.

SUPERVISOR: Those are all great ideas. Which one would you like to try this next week?

COACH: I want to try writing a note for each teacher and leaving it with the teacher.

SUPERVISOR: When do you plan to write the notes?

COACH: I want to try writing them during my observation. If that doesn't work, I'll write them right after our coaching conversations.

SUPERVISOR: Let me know how it goes. Let's move on to C2: Communicate Shared Goals. What was your self-reflection for this section?

COACH: I introduced the new focus area: promoting children's higher-level thinking skills. Willie reflected on her current practices, and we came up with some additional strategies and made a new shared goal. I forgot to follow up on the goals from our last coaching session. I need to write myself a note so I remember.

SUPERVISOR: That's where the planning sheet can help you. It's sometimes hard for teachers and coaches to remember what they discussed at the last coaching session. What could you do to remind Willie and yourself about your shared goals?

COACH: I could contact her a few days before our coaching session and remind her that we'll be discussing her progress on the goals.

SUPERVISOR: Yes, and one of other steps in C3 is to set up a check-in date. That's when you have the teacher share with you when she plans to work on the goal, and then you follow up in between coaching sessions. The sooner the teacher works on the shared goal after your coaching session, the more likely it is that she'll actually follow through, especially if there's a plan for checking in.

COACH: True. I need to remember to set a check-in date.

SUPERVISOR: I liked how you introduced the new area of focus—promoting children's higher-level thinking skills—and had Willie reflect. You worked effectively together to create your new shared goal. She seemed engaged during the process.

COACH: Thanks. Willie did seem excited about the new goal.

SUPERVISOR: Let's continue to look at C3. What's your reflection on this section?

COACH: I know I struggled in this section. What would you suggest?

SUPERVISOR: Let's break it down step by step. The shared goal was "To promote children's higher-level thinking skills in the block area by having the children make predictions." So the desired outcome was "To promote children's higher-level thinking skills in the block area," and the strategy was "Having the children make predictions." You can check the teacher's understanding of both the desired outcome and the strategy. What questions could you ask to see if Willie understood?

COACH: I could ask her to explain what higher-level thinking skills are and to give some examples of how to promote those skills.

SUPERVISOR: Yes, you can have the teacher define the desired outcome, the skill that it includes, and the strategy; you can also have her give examples to demonstrate her understanding. You did complete the next two steps, which were to ask Willie to explain why the desired outcome was important and to flesh out the strategy by identifying when, where, and with whom she would teach the skill. The next step is to model the strategy. How could you do that?

COACH: I really don't know.

SUPERVISOR: How could you develop ideas for modeling?

COACH: I could develop a plan before I go coaching and also talk to other coaches about what they do.

SUPERVISOR: Those are both good ideas. Let's think about how you could engage a teacher in modeling. What if you pretended to be Willie and she pretended to be a child playing in the block area? You could model asking the child to make a prediction. Then you could reverse roles so Willie could practice.

COACH: Okay, but it feels kind of awkward role-playing.

SUPERVISOR: It will at first, but with time, you'll see the benefits of having teachers practice strategies. It also gives you more opportunities to check their understanding.

COACH: I'll give it a try.

SUPERVISOR: Good. I'd like you to give me a report after your next coaching session. To increase your comfort level, let's practice right now. If we practice a couple of times, you may feel more comfortable with modeling and practicing in an actual coaching conversation. First, I'll model. I want you to pretend to be a child in the block area. I'll be the teacher. Petra, I noticed that you're building a really tall tower.

COACH: (*Pretending to be a child.*) Yes, I'm building a tower so tall it'll touch the ceiling.

SUPERVISOR: Wow! That'd be a really tall tower. What do you think will happen if you build a tower all the way to the ceiling?

COACH: (*As a child.*) I think it'd fall down.

SUPERVISOR: How could you make it sturdy enough to not fall down?

COACH: (*As a child.*) I could make it bigger.

SUPERVISOR: Why would making it bigger make it sturdy enough to not fall down?

COACH: (*As a child.*) It'd be thicker.

SUPERVISOR: You're right; it would be thicker. Good thinking. Okay, let's stop. Now it's your turn. I want you to be the teacher, and I'll be the child—only this time, think of a slightly different scenario.

COACH: How about we pretend you're making a bridge in the block area?

SUPERVISOR: Sounds good. (*Starts pretending to build a bridge with blocks.*)

COACH: Teresa, what are you making?

SUPERVISOR: (*Pretending to be a child.*) I'm making a long bridge.

COACH: Why are you making a long bridge?

SUPERVISOR: (*As a child.*) I want to drive all my cars way over there.

COACH: Why do you want to drive all your cars way over there?

SUPERVISOR: (*As a child.*): They like it over there.

COACH: It looks like a great place to go. What do you need to make your long bridge?

SUPERVISOR: (*As a child.*): I need more blocks!

COACH: Let's go find some more blocks.

SUPERVISOR: All right, let's stop there. How did it feel to do the role play?

COACH: It went better than I thought it would. What if a teacher doesn't want to role-play?

SUPERVISOR: I think your positive attitude and encouragement will help the teacher feel comfortable. You may want to confess that you feel a little uncomfortable role-playing too, and then you can say, "But together, we'll make it fun."

COACH: I think if I make it fun, we'll both feel more comfortable.

SUPERVISOR: Also remember to have the teacher reflect on how the strategy will make a difference in the children's lives. Then set a specific date for having the teacher complete and report on the plan of action.

COACH: Okay, I will.

SUPERVISOR: I thought you did a nice job of partnering with Willie. You've developed a positive rapport with her, and she seemed very comfortable during your coaching session. Any questions on the C3 section?

COACH: No, I know what to do now. I'll use the planning sheet, and that'll help me stay on track and do all the steps.

SUPERVISOR: Good idea. Let's move to C4: Closing Connections. Share your thoughts on this section with me.

COACH: I thanked Willie for her time, and I encouraged her to work on the new goal and asked her to reflect on her teaching practices. I forgot to ask her if she had any questions, but I did tell her what our next focus area would be and when we were going to meet again.

SUPERVISOR: Yes, you made some great closing connections. What could you do for next time to help you remember to ask if the teacher has any questions?

COACH: I'll make sure I use the planning sheet and check off each item as I go along.

SUPERVISOR: Good plan. For the coaching session you had today, you could follow up with an email asking Willie if she has any questions.

COACH: That's a good idea. I'll do that.

SUPERVISOR: Would you like to share your glows and grows?

COACH: One *glow* and *grow* is that I shared lots of strengths with Willie, but because I took so much time on that, I didn't have time for everything else. So one of my grows is to share just one powerful glow during the coaching conversation and write a note to the teacher sharing some of the other glows I observed. Another glow that I wrote down was my positive relationship with Willie. She seemed very comfortable meeting with me. I thought we did a great job of coming up with a shared goal and completing a plan of action. My other grows are to outline the coaching conversation, to start modeling and practicing with the teacher, and to give the teacher more time to reflect. I noticed I was doing most of the talking, and I need to give each teacher more time to reflect and share her thoughts and ideas. I also need to remember to set check-in dates so teachers can report on what they've done.

SUPERVISOR: Let's recap our conversation. Your glows were showing enthusiasm, giving Willie lots of positive feedback, successfully partnering with her to create a plan of action, and making meaningful closing connections. You also shared several grows. What would you like to work on during the next couple of weeks?

COACH: I really want to work on giving an overview of the coaching conversation and making sure I ask the teacher for her feedback before I give my positive feedback. I'm also going to limit my glows during the coaching conversation, write a few of them down on a note card, and leave it with the teacher. I want to think more about how to model and practice during the conversation. Can we meet again in a few days and talk over my ideas?

SUPERVISOR: That's a great idea. Let's meet again on Thursday at 2:00 p.m. Will that work for you?

COACH: Yes, that'll work.

SUPERVISOR: Thank you for meeting with me. I look forward to hearing about your progress and ideas for modeling and practicing when we meet on Thursday. Do you have any questions?

COACH: No, I'll see you on Thursday. Thanks!

Lessons from the Conversation

This conversation demonstrates several important principles for coaching coaches with the RSBC Model:

- The coach, like the real person on whom she is based, has a talent for identifying teachers' strengths. She loves to share lots of positive feedback—it makes teachers happy, and she feels good about it. This step is important, but sometimes a short, simple statement is more powerful than five minutes of positive feedback. Teachers need time to internalize feedback and reflect on how their own teaching practices make a difference in the lives of children (hopefully for the better).

- The CRT provides a basis for discussion, and the coach identifies many of her own opportunities for growth based on what she has discovered by completing the form. The supervisor provides additional training and support in areas that need work. For instance, the coach recognizes that she tends to focus on the steps that she feels most comfortable with and tends to skip steps that are less comfortable (a common tactic among new coaches). The supervisor addresses this issue by taking time to model and practice with the coach.

- Did you notice how the supervisor is slow to give answers to the coach's questions and often asks the coach to answer them herself? Self-discovery is a powerful technique for promoting learning and development.

- After coaching conversations, supervisors need to follow up with coaches just as much as coaches need to follow up with teachers. In this case, the coach takes the initiative to set up another meeting with the supervisor to go over modeling and practicing. As coaches become more proficient in implementing the RSBC Model, they may not need as many supervisor observations or feedback sessions. However, supervisors should continue to conduct periodic checks, as practices tend to slide with time. Coaches also appreciate receiving positive feedback from supervisors, and meeting together provides time to build relationships and for supervisors to gain a greater appreciation for the work that coaches do.

MODIFYING THE RSBC MODEL

You may already have thought of twenty different ways to change and adapt the RSBC Model to meet your unique situation. You might even have ideas for improving the model. That is one thing I love about early childhood professionals: they are always thinking of ways to make things even better. The important thing is to find what works best for you, whether as a coach or as a supervisor. I hope you can take some of these ideas and tools and use them within your coaching initiatives.

PART 3

FACILITATING EFFECTIVE
TRAINING SESSIONS

CHAPTER 9:

Teaching Adult Learners

Felicity is excited to attend a training session called Math in the Preschool Classroom. She hopes she will gain ideas to spark children's interest in math. But the instructor begins by blandly reciting the state math standards and proceeds to read every word on his PowerPoint. When someone tries to ask a question, he brushes it off and continues his lecture. Felicity can't wait for the class to end!

When Andre arrives at a different session of Math in the Preschool Classroom, the instructor invites participants to interact with the manipulatives on their tables before class begins. Then the instructor encourages participants to discuss what they did with the materials and any math skills they used, such as sorting or creating patterns. Later, participants partner up to read and discuss case studies about implementing state math standards. Near the end of the session, small groups share the strategies they use to teach preschool math skills. Andre leaves feeling energized and ready to incorporate some new math ideas into his own classroom.

Oliver Wendell Holmes Sr. stated, "Every now and then a man's mind is stretched by a new idea . . . and never shrinks back to its former dimensions." If you are a trainer, you serve as a facilitator of PL, striving to stretch and expand learners' understanding. However, as any early childhood professional can attest (and as many trainers can ruefully admit), training sessions can sometimes turn out to be excruciatingly dull, largely irrelevant, or both. This chapter explores how adults learn and how you can use this knowledge to make your training sessions both interesting to and useful for your audiences.

TRAITS OF ADULT LEARNERS

To teach adults effectively, trainers need to understand the traits of adult learners. In one training session, I asked participants to respond to the prompts "Adult learners are . . ." and "Adult learners need . . ." The group provided some revealing answers:

Adult learners are . . .

- Unique

- Strongly motivated

- Human beings with dreams, goals, and feelings

- Individuals with different experiences

- Each an expert on something

- Seeking to improve themselves

Adult learners need . . .

- Encouragement

- Hands-on training

- Support and reinforcement

- Engagement and interaction

- To be open to learn

- Different ways to approach an idea and learn a topic

- Training topics that are meaningful to them

Take a few moments to thoughtfully reflect on these insightful responses. The two lists remind us that adult learners need various approaches to learning, not one-size-fits-all training. Furthermore, every adult is an expert on something. A trainer needs to take the role of a respectful partner and honor adult learners' expertise.

The comment "Adult learners are human beings with dreams, goals, and feelings" particularly resonated with me because trainers provide a strong source of encouragement and support for adult learners. Trainers can inspire their audiences to learn and grow as professionals. Take a moment to think of a teacher or mentor who believed in you. Contemplate how that person helped you along your professional journey. The following experience illustrates how important these relationships can be.

As a young professional, I served on a state board for a professional organization. The president of the board took a special interest in me and saw things in me that I did not see in myself. She said to me, "One day, you are going to be the president of this board and lead the profession in a positive direction." Her belief in me gave me the courage to run for a national office on the student board of the organization. I was elected secretary and had an amazing experience serving as a national officer.

Now think about your role as a trainer. You serve as a teacher and role model to early childhood professionals, even if you only meet them once. What opportunities do you have to inspire and encourage others to do and be more than they currently think is possible?

In 2004, NAEYC adopted the "Code of Ethical Conduct: Supplement for Early Childhood Adult Educators." This document provides ideals, principles, and guidance for adult educators who work with early childhood professionals. I encourage you to read the complete supplement and incorporate applicable ideas into your practice (available at https://www.naeyc.org/sites/default/files/globally-shared/downloads/ PDFs/resources/position-statements/ethics04_09202013update.pdf).

MASLOW'S HIERARCHY OF NEEDS AND ADULT LEARNERS

Along with unique traits, adult learners have universal human needs. Psychologist Abraham Maslow created a well-known hierarchy that identifies five levels of needs (listed from lowest level to highest):

- Physiological needs (such as food, water, and shelter)

- Safety needs (such as security and stability)

- Love and belonging needs (such as friendship and trust)

- Esteem needs (such as achievement and status)

- Self-actualization needs (such as self-fulfillment)

Usually, individuals must satisfy their lower-level needs before they can address their higher-level needs. If you have ever struggled to concentrate during a staff meeting because you had skipped lunch or were worried about driving home in worsening weather, you have seen this principle in action.

Maslow's hierarchy has important implications for teaching adult learners. Let's examine how you can use this theory to improve your training sessions.

PHYSIOLOGICAL NEEDS

Adult learners want an environment with comfortable seating and just the right temperature. They also function better if they have sufficient food and rest. Remember, it is hard to learn when you are hungry, tired, or uncomfortable! Think about your training space and whether it promotes optimum learning, and ask yourself the following questions:

- Is the furniture adult sized?

- Can I control the temperature?

- Can participants bring food to the training session?

- Do I have breaks built into the schedule?

- What else can I do to meet participants' physiological needs?

Granted, some of these things might be out of your control. If the air conditioning is not working properly or the building policy prohibits food and drinks in the meeting room, you will need to do your best to meet adult learners' physiological needs. Ask yourself, "What is within my control?" For instance, regardless of technical difficulties or building policies, you can build breaks into the schedule and make participants as comfortable as possible.

SAFETY NEEDS

A positive, welcoming atmosphere helps to establish an emotionally safe environment for learning. Ask yourself the following questions:

• Is my training environment emotionally safe?

• Will participants feel comfortable asking questions and discussing topics with each other?

• How do I respond to comments and questions?

• Do I speak encouraging words and display unbiased actions?

• What else can I do to meet participants' safety needs?

LOVE AND BELONGING NEEDS

Individuals want to belong and feel accepted for who they are. Trainers can establish a community of learners by building connections and feelings of belonging. Ask yourself the following questions:

• How can I maintain respect within the group?

• How can I encourage participants to become friends?

• What playful activities can I incorporate to foster feelings of unity?

• What else can I do to meet participants' love and belonging needs?

ESTEEM NEEDS

Adults meet their esteem needs by achieving goals and receiving recognition. Ask yourself the following questions:

• Does my training schedule include time for setting goals or creating plans of action?

• How can I enable participants to share their accomplishments?

• How can I acknowledge participants' progress and recognize their growth and development?

• What else can I do to meet participants' esteem needs?

SELF-ACTUALIZATION NEEDS

Self-actualization involves finding fulfillment and pursuing creative activities. Self-actualization generally happens after participants leave a training session and begin implementing new skills and practices, but trainers can still assist in this process. Ask yourself the following questions:

• How can I provide opportunities for participants to be creative during the training session?

• What tools can I give participants to help them measure their success as they implement new skills and practices?

• What are some ways that participants could share the results of implementing new skills and practices?

• What else can I do to meet participants' self-actualization needs?

HELPING ADULT LEARNERS MEET THEIR NEEDS

Trainers should strive to help meet adult learners' physiological, safety, belonging, esteem, and self-actualization needs. Furthermore, trainers and adult learners should collaborate to create ways for leaners to take care of these needs for themselves and others. Trainers can remind adult learners about Maslow's hierarchy and have them discuss ways that they can meet their own needs and others' needs. For example, adult learners can take care of their self-actualization needs by focusing on the topic at hand and can take care of others' love and belonging needs by listening to differing points of view.

ADULT LEARNING PRINCIPLES

Having discussed the traits and needs of adult learners, we can now look at how to teach them. As trainers, we want to inspire change and help adult learners progress in their professional growth, but sometimes our efforts are not welcomed. Compared to children, adult learners are sometimes less open-minded and more resistant to change. After all, changing behavior and attitudes is hard. To help adult learners desire to change, trainers need to understand how adults learn and what matters to them.

In their book *The Adult Learner: The Definitive Classic in Adult Education and Human Resource Development*, Malcolm Knowles, Elwood Holton III, and Richard Swanson present six principles for teaching adult learners. By following these principles as you prepare and carry out PL sessions, you can ensure that your sessions engage learners and are relevant to their needs.

PRINCIPLE 1: THE LEARNER'S NEED TO KNOW

Adult learners have an innate need to know why they need to learn something. Once they understand why, they are ready to understand what and how they will learn. Explaining the what, why, and how of learning promotes buy-in by helping adults realize how PL content relates to their lives.

> How can you meet adult learners' need to know?

You can follow this first principle by helping learners understand how theoretical concepts apply to real situations. To make these connections, ask reflective questions that draw on participants' wisdom and experience. Ask participants reflective questions, such as, "How have you built strong relationships with the families of the children in your classroom?" Then listen as participants share their experiences.

Adults appreciate understanding the "what, so what, and now what" of learning. These three simple questions are based on the reflective model proposed by Gary Rolfe, Dawn Freshwater, and Melanie Jasper. The "what" explains what participants will learn, the "so what" tells why that information is important, and the "now what" describes how to apply the information. For example, a trainer could say, "You'll be learning about how to use scientific inquiry in preschool classrooms [the 'what']. Scientific inquiry gives children opportunities to solve problems and develop critical thinking skills [the 'so what']. You can apply the information you learn today in your classroom—for example, you can help a child form a hypothesis about why his block tower fell over [the 'now what']."

PRINCIPLE 2: SELF-CONCEPT OF THE LEARNER

Adults see themselves as having significant autonomy in their own lives, and they want the same kind of control over their learning. They need ownership of learning goals and purposes. They also prefer to be self-directed and proactive in the learning process. By taking on these responsibilities, adults gain deeper understanding of themselves.

> How can you help adult learners be self-directed?

To follow this principle, involve adult learners in decisions about the content and process of learning. For example, if a training session focuses on supporting language development, discuss specific subtopics of language development that interest the learners. You could also give participants a choice about whether to complete an assignment by writing a paper, giving a presentation, or creating a visual. Rather than dictating everything that they must do, honor adult learners' desires to be independent and self-directed.

PRINCIPLE 3: PRIOR EXPERIENCE OF THE LEARNER

Adults bring prior experience to the learning environment. They already have mental models that explain how things work in the real world. Their collective wealth of expertise provides an important resource for you as a trainer. Take advantage of it by incorporating it into the learning process. When designing training sessions, build in time for holding discussions and sharing ideas. Throughout a session, ask participants questions such as, "How would you say that in your own words?" or "Can you give us an example from your classroom?" Use case studies to help learners make connections to prior learning. When learners read and discuss scenarios similar to their own situations, they can better understand how to use what they have learned.

Additionally, provide opportunities for learners to evaluate, reflect on, and review their own experiences. For instance, during a training session that I led for a group of child-care-center directors, we discussed the power of filming teachers in their classrooms and using the videos as part of coaching. One of the directors became quite excited. She explained that she watched videos of her teachers every day but that she had never thought of using video as a coaching tool. She could hardly wait to go back to her center and use her videos in a new way.

> How can you use adult learners' past experiences as a resource for learning?

One cautionary note related to prior experience: adult learners also have biases, assumptions, and personal goals that may cause them to resist learning new content and practices. As you gain more experience and discover common objections to your ideas, update your training presentations to address those issues. For example, you might say, "I know that what I'm presenting may be different from what you're currently doing in your classroom. But I want you to be open to new ideas as I illustrate ways that other teachers have used these strategies in their classrooms. As we go along, I want you to share your concerns and also your ideas on how these strategies could be adapted for your classroom." When adult learners feel that trainers understand their concerns and have brainstormed solutions, they become more willing to consider ways that they can adopt the ideas from training sessions into their own classrooms.

PRINCIPLE 4: READINESS TO LEARN

This principle is closely correlated with Principle 1. Adults have a higher commitment to learning when they are faced with immediate need. For them, relevancy trumps everything. They want PL that can help them with what they currently do in their jobs or personal lives. If the content is not relevant to them, adults are not interested. But when life experiences create a need to know, adults become ready to learn. For instance, when a child throws blocks in the classroom, his teacher becomes much more interested in and ready to learn about positive-guidance techniques. When a new dual-language learner joins a classroom, his teacher becomes much more interested in ideas for teaching dual-language learners.

> How you can tap into adult learners' readiness to learn?

Much as you do when honoring participants' need to know, you can tap into adult learners' readiness to learn by helping them understand how concepts apply to their current situations. Stories, videos, and real-life examples powerfully illustrate how PL can be useful outside of a training session. For example, a teacher whom I'll call Emma was having difficulty understanding how to help young children deal with strong emotions. After hearing a story about what a trainer had done in the past in her own classroom, Emma came up with several ideas for what to do in her classroom.

PRINCIPLE 5: ORIENTATION TO LEARNING

Orientation to learning relates to how adults prefer to learn. Adult learners prefer educational content that focuses on tasks or problems rather than theories. They want to solve problems and prevent future issues. They are more open to change if they understand why that change will benefit the children in their classrooms. In particular, adult learners want content with immediate applicability—things they can take back to their classrooms and implement tomorrow.

> How can you provide immediacy of application for adult learners'?

You can follow this principle by providing opportunities for adult learners to collectively solve problems that they currently face in their jobs. Look for ways to have participants actively practice new skills and test their new knowledge. For example, one effective engagement strategy is to provide learners with realistic case studies that they can discuss and determine potential solutions for.

PRINCIPLE 6: MOTIVATION TO LEARN

Adults are internally motivated to learn. They generally engage in PL in search of intangible personal benefits, such as increased job satisfaction or quality of life, rather than grades, prizes, or other external rewards. You can follow this principle by helping adult learners understand how new knowledge and practices will benefit them and their students. Share ways that the information applies both personally and professionally. For instance, during a

> What can you do to tap into adult learners' internal motivation?

training session on ways to help children calm down, one teacher noted that several of the ideas could also help him when he felt frustrated or upset. It is always fun when you are training on communication techniques and a training participant mentions that he needs to try the ideas with his significant other!

FIXED OR GROWTH MINDSET?

Even when trainers understand the traits of adult learners, help meet participants' needs, and follow the adult learning principles, some adult learners struggle to believe that they can make changes and succeed in a learning environment. These learners have difficulty with their *mindsets*—their ways of thinking about their potential and abilities. According to Carol Dweck, author of *Mindset: The New Psychology of Success*, learners fall into two categories: people with a fixed mindset and people with a growth mindset.

FIXED MINDSET

Someone with a fixed mindset believes that each person is born with a certain amount of intelligence and potential. Thus, a person's abilities (such as intellectual, athletic, or musical) are set. He may be able to learn new things, but he can only progress so far because his talents have innate limits.

People with fixed mindsets seek to look smart, so they reject tasks if they think they might make mistakes. They tend to conceal problems and any errors that they make. Their egos are connected to their performances—if they fail, they feel bad about themselves.

GROWTH MINDSET

In contrast, people with a growth mindset believe that anyone can work hard to increase his potential and intelligence. A person can develop his artistic ability, athleticism, business skills, or any other proficiency. Just as importantly, performance can consistently improve over time.

Individuals with growth mindsets seek out challenging tasks and are open to making mistakes. They believe that mistakes provide one way to learn and grow. Their egos are connected to their efforts—they accept failure but not laziness in themselves.

Interestingly, the same person (including you) can have both a growth mindset and a fixed mindset at the same time. For example, a person might have a growth mindset about his artistic ability and a fixed mindset about his athletic ability. Ideally, a person develops a growth mindset in all aspects of his life.

CHANGING FROM A FIXED MINDSET TO A GROWTH MINDSET

Trainers benefit from having a growth mindset about both themselves and adult learners. Dweck points out that people change fixed mindsets into growth mindsets by following these steps:

1. Recognize the fixed-mindset voice—the voice in your head that says, "You can't do it," and "You might fail, so you'd better not try."

2. Decide whether to believe the voice.

3. Talk back to the fixed-mindset voice with a growth-mindset voice. For example, say to yourself, "I may not be able to do it now, but I can learn to do it with time and effort."

4. Act in ways that demonstrate your willingness to work hard and make mistakes.

Think about some adult learners you know. Can you identify times when they had fixed mindsets? What about times when they had growth mindsets? How has each mindset affected their abilities to learn and to grow?

Often our personal thoughts can influence our mindsets. If I say to myself, "I am not good at this," or "I give up! This is too hard," I have much lower chances of success because my thoughts encourage a fixed mindset. In contrast, if I say to myself, "I'm not good at this *yet*," and "This may take more time and effort, but I will learn it in time," I feed a growth mindset and am more likely to succeed because of my willingness to keep trying.

We can learn from the examples of famous people who had growth mindsets. According to writer Jennifer Latson in *Time* magazine, inventor Thomas Edison had over six thousand unsuccessful attempts when developing the first affordable electric lightbulb. Biographers Frank Dyer and Thomas Martin report that when someone commented on Edison's lack of results, Edison answered, "Why, man, I have gotten a lot of results! I know several thousand things that won't work." He is an example of true persistence!

As another example, Michael Jordan is considered one of the best basketball players of all time. However, a famous commercial (quoted by Eric Zorn of the *Chicago Tribune*) points out that over his career, Jordan lost nearly three hundred games and missed more than nine thousand shots, including twenty-six that could have sealed victory for his team. But Jordan demonstrated his growth mindset by not giving up. "I've failed over and over and over again in my life," the commercial declares. "And that is why I succeed." Indeed, failure is part of the road to success.

You may be tempted to think, "Well, that's all well and good for famous people like Thomas Edison and Michael Jordan. But what about regular people like me?" Carol Dweck's work provides some powerful insights about mindset in everyday people. In one of her studies, fifth-graders individually completed both easy and hard puzzles. When a student finished, the researchers either told him that he was smart or praised him for his efforts and hard work. Then the researchers offered the student a choice: he could complete another easy puzzle or another hard puzzle. Interestingly, the majority of "smart" students chose easy puzzles, while the majority of "hardworking" students chose hard puzzles. Dweck concluded that the different types of praise influenced whether the students had fixed mindsets or growth mindsets. This makes sense: to a child, a person is either smart or not smart (an idea that leads to a fixed mindset), but a person can put forth varying degrees of effort (an idea that leads to a growth mindset).

Likewise, the type of feedback that trainers give adult learners can influence whether the learners gravitate to fixed mindsets or growth mindsets. You can model a growth mindset with your words and actions. As you use phrases such as "You can do it," and "Keep trying—it'll come," you promote a growth mindset. By giving feedback focused on efforts (such as "I can see that you're working hard to resolve this problem. There's more than one way to solve it"), you shift the focus from obtaining the "right" answer to discovering multiple solutions. You can also teach adult learners to listen to their growth-mindset voices and act accordingly. Teach adult learners to add growth-mindset phrases (such as, "I won't give up. I can solve this," and "I can use a different strategy. What else could I try?") to their thought patterns. It takes time and effort to change our mindsets, but the results can have powerful effects on us and on others.

CHAPTER 10:

Meeting the Needs of Diverse Learners

Anya is deaf in one ear. Before attending a training session, she explains to Heather, the instructor, that she (Anya) needs to sit in the front row and needs Heather to speak directly to her so that Anya can hear and read Heather's lips if needed. At the training session, Heather keeps her body oriented toward Anya. During breaks, Heather checks in with Anya to make sure that she can hear and understands what is being said. Heather also prints out her presentation script for Anya so that she can reference the main points and follow along.

So far, we have looked at factors in training sessions that are or should be essentially the same for all adult learners. However, just as children do, adult learners have a variety of unique characteristics that affect the training environment. As a trainer, you must learn to recognize, appreciate, and honor the diversity of the people who attend your training sessions. Effective trainers understand the many ways in which characteristics such as learning preferences, generational differences, culture, language, and abilities can influence a training session. You will need to prepare to respond to these factors in positive, supportive ways.

LEARNING PREFERENCES

Adult learners differ in how they prefer to have content presented to them. For example, in Sarah Bradway's short video "Vision of an Adult Learner Today," various adult learners display phrases that explain how they prefer to learn. For instance, one student writes on a whiteboard, "I do *not* learn from lecture," while another student holds up a sign that says, "I learn best by reading and discussion." One of my favorite moments occurs when one student holds up a sign that reads, "I *hate* PowerPoints"—and the next student holds up a sign that reads, "I *love* PowerPoints."

This example illustrates how adult learners have diverse preferences when it comes to learning. What one person loves about PL, another person may dislike. These distinct learning needs can create difficulties for trainers, especially if they do not yet know the learning preferences of the people they will teach. One way to address this challenge is to diversify the learning experience.

Try using a variety of each of these elements:

• media (such as manipulatives or videos)

• formats (such as written handouts or verbal instructions)

• activities (such as holding discussions or creating visuals)

In addition, provide adult learners with opportunities to share and learn from each other, such as by using the following strategy. As a bonus, this activity also helps you discover your participants' learning preferences.

Engagement Strategy: Silent Sign Sharing

Materials

1 sheet of unlined paper per participant

pens or pencils

1. Pass out a sheet of paper (and a pen or pencil, if needed) to each participant.

2. Provide a prompt, such as, "I learn by . . ." **Tip:** Create a prompt related to the topic of your training session.

3. Have participants create signs with their answers, writing large enough for others to read.

4. Instruct learners to walk around the room, silently showing their signs to others.

5. Once everyone has seen all the signs, you can either have the participants discuss their signs in small groups or lead a whole-group discussion on what participants learned by reading the signs.

In my experience, learners often comment on the similarities and differences they noticed.

GENERATIONAL DIFFERENCES

Not only do adult learners bring individual learning preferences to a training session, but they represent many different age groups. For the first time in history, there can be employees from as many as five different generations at the same workplace. Likewise, there can be up to five generations of adult learners in the same training session. Sometimes special challenges arise when teaching multiple generations at the same time. You may have experienced some of these challenges if, for example, you have ever made a pop-culture reference during a training session and gotten a few laughs but many more blank stares. The term *generation gap* exists for a reason!

What causes these difficulties? One major factor is that individuals are influenced by life events. These experiences shape our attitudes and influence our outlooks. Some especially powerful occurrences, such as national and world events and media influences, can shape entire generations.

What do you think? Do you agree? Think back to the media, events, and people that influenced you during your formative years. Did you grow up in the 1960s and experience the Space Race and watch the first man walk on the moon? Did you grow up in the 1980s and witness the

Challenger explosion and the fall of the Berlin Wall? Consider how your experiences affected who you are today. How did they shape the way you view people and make sense of the world?

GENERATION INFORMATION

It is helpful for trainers to understand some of the unique events that members of each generation experienced during their formative years. Collectively, you may notice certain distinctive characteristics among adult learners based on when they grew up. These patterns make it tempting to stereotype people by generation. However, people also adapt and change as they grow and as their environments change. Remember that individual preferences always outweigh generational preferences.

Different researchers have given a variety of labels and chronological boundaries to generations. For our purposes, we will use the generational categories and timeline from the book *When Generations Collide* by Lynne Lancaster and David Stillman:

• Traditionalists: born 1900–1945

• Baby Boomers: born 1946–1964

• Generation X: born 1965–1980

• Millennials (sometimes called Generation Y): born 1981–1999

• Generation Z or Generation 2020: born 2000–2020

Because most living Traditionalists have now retired and because information about Generation Z in the workplace is just beginning to emerge, this book does not discuss either of these generations. Instead, let's briefly examine the other three generations.

Baby Boomers

Baby Boomers (born 1946–1964) grew up among many tumultuous events, including the Space Race, the Civil Rights Movement, the Vietnam War, the Watergate scandal, and Woodstock. After World War II, the United States experienced a tremendous baby boom: 76 million births in nineteen years, according to Kelvin Pollard and Paola Scommegna of the Population Reference Bureau. Society was not prepared for all these children, so many new hospitals and schools needed to be built. It was a competitive but generally affluent and productive time. During these years, television became widespread, giving people the ability to view events happening in distant locations. For instance, television enabled many Baby Boomers to watch the assassination of President John F. Kennedy and its aftermath, events that left indelible impressions on these young people. Nonetheless, the media also reflected the optimism of society with shows such as *Walt Disney Presents*. Popular artists included Elvis Presley, the Beach Boys, and Simon and Garfunkel.

Individuals born close to a generation boundary are sometimes called "Cuspers," as they are born on the cusp of two different generations and often have characteristics of both generations.

In the workplace, Baby Boomers have a strong work ethic. Many people from this generation are competitive, driven, and hardworking. They are often team oriented and love attending meetings and being on committees. They are interested in personal growth and achievement.

Generation X

Generation X, or Gen X (born 1965–1980), grew up amid double-digit inflation, an AIDS epidemic in the United States, and the Gulf War. This generation saw the *Challenger* explode and the Berlin Wall fall. During this period, the divorce rate tripled, and many young people became so-called latchkey children because their parents worked outside the home. Gen Xers were also influenced by early video games. Other media from this generation included *Friends, Seinfeld,* and *The Simpsons.*

In the workplace, Gen Xers tend to be flexible, resourceful, and very self-reliant. They are realists and are unafraid to ask for the reasons behind policies and procedures. They think globally and are more technologically literate than previous generations. Because of recession, global competition, and Baby Boomers' not retiring, many Gen Xers have not had opportunities to become leaders in the traditional workplace. Recession has also caused many Gen Xers to lose their jobs and become entrepreneurs instead.

Millennials

Millennials (born 1981–1999) grew up witnessing the Oklahoma City bombing, 9/11, the Great Recession, and the election of President Barack Obama. (Note that although 9/11 changed the world for all generations, it arguably had the deepest impact on Millennials because they were so young when it occurred.) Part of this generation includes a second baby boom: approximately 80 million births between 1982 and 1995, as Vivian Marino of *The New York Times* estimates. Parents were very involved with their Millennial children, and Millennials regularly seek parental advice even after leaving home. Top media for Millennials included shows such as *Survivor, CSI,* and *ER* and a diverse range of music from artists such as Beyoncé, Eminem, Usher, and Boyz II Men.

Younger Millennials are technology natives. Craig Smith of DMR Business Statistics states that 92 percent of Millennials own smartphones. According to a study by the Pew Research Center, 83 percent of Millennials sleep with or near their smartphones, and 88 percent of Millennials use their cell phones for texting (compared to 51 percent of Baby Boomers).

Millennials utilize this technological savvy in the workplace. They expect open communication and want to be taken seriously. Despite their confidence, they like frequent feedback from supervisors. Millennials prefer to work in teams, seeing group-based work as more fun and less risky. They like to multitask and often think outside the box. They are a diverse and educated generation desiring innovative, creative, meaningful work that makes a difference.

ADDRESSING GENERATIONAL DIFFERENCES

As we have seen, members of each generation bring unique life experiences to the training environment. Remember that these experiences cause adult learners to have different attitudes, values, and practices. You can apply this knowledge of generational differences to create positive PL events for all adult learners:

• **Use their experiences.** Be aware of the vast variety of experiences within a group of adult learners. Honor their experiences and encourage participants to share them.

- **Take advantage of their strengths.** Plan ways to utilize the strengths and values of different generations. For instance, incorporate technology into your PL sessions to highlight the strengths of Millennials and Gen X. Allow Baby Boomers to shine as they share their vast experience and demonstrate skills in team-building activities.

- **Vary your methods.** As mentioned earlier, use multiple instruction techniques, such as videos and discussions. The tools of learning have changed dramatically over generations, from books for Baby Boomers to voice-activated search engines for Millennials. By varying your methods, you help adult learners stay engaged, feel secure (because they recognize the formats you are using), and perhaps learn to use new or less-familiar educational tools.

- **Be patient with learners and technology.** Recognize that some adult learners, regardless of generation, struggle with certain types of technology. For instance, if you use an online game or poll, some learners may have difficulty participating, so consider pairing participants based on their abilities and strengths.

- **Remember context.** Acknowledge that each adult learner's values and attitudes about caring for and teaching children will be influenced by the time and manner in which that person was brought up. Some learners were reared by extremely controlling parents, while other learners' parents were much more lenient and allowed greater autonomy and self-expression. The way an individual was brought up influences how she believes that children should be taught.

- **Perhaps most importantly, let them grow.** Avoid assuming that adult learners will always think and act in certain ways because of the generations they come from. Even seemingly set-in-their-ways adults can continue to be influenced by their experiences and change for the better. For example, as a Baby Boomer, I initially resisted texting my staff instead of calling or emailing them. But I adapted to texting and actually learned to prefer it for some types of messages

In any type of PL, but especially when participants come from multiple generations, trainers need to encourage connections among adult learners. Try this engagement strategy to help learners from different generations connect with each other.

Engagement Strategy: Coin Conversation Starters
Materials

1 coin per participant (participants can use their own)

1. Direct the participants to each take out a coin and find the year in which it was minted. For this activity, each participant should choose a coin with a year during which she was alive and old enough to remember things.

2. Briefly explain to the participants the names and birth-year ranges for each generation. It may help to make a PowerPoint slide with this information ahead of time so the participants can refer to it during the activity.

3. Have the participants form groups of three. If possible, no more than two group members should be from the same generation.

4. Instruct group members to discuss these questions with each other:

- How old were you in the year on your coin?

- What do you remember about that year?

- What significant events happened in your life and in the world that year?

- What music, movies, and television shows do you remember from that year? (If necessary, participants can search the internet to jog their memories.)

- How did the media, events, and people from this time of your life influence who you are today?

5. Bring the large group back together and discuss some of the insights from the small-group conversations.

CULTURE

Culture refers to the knowledge, shared experiences, values, beliefs, attitudes, and roles acquired by a group of people over many generations. It also includes behaviors cultivated through social learning and interactions within the group, such as whether a person expresses concerns openly (direct communication, preferred in mainstream American culture) or only hints at them to avoid giving offense (indirect communication, preferred in many Asian cultures).

Culture influences how people view the world, so it matters a great deal to individuals. Cultural differences can also become sources of confusion or conflict if poorly navigated—for example, Gayle Cotton of the *Huffington Post* explains that depending on culture, an upraised thumb can show approval, be used for counting, or form an extremely rude gesture. Therefore, to make training sessions positive and effective for all adult learners, trainers need to become *culturally responsive*. According to Lucy Williams's article "How to Accept and Respect Other Cultures," cultural responsiveness includes having an openness to the viewpoints, thoughts, and experiences of others as you learn from and interact respectfully with them.

WHY BEING CULTURALLY RESPONSIVE MATTERS

Two core values of the early childhood profession are equity and opportunity. The "About Us" page of the NAEYC website declares, "We advance a diverse, dynamic early childhood profession and support all who care for, educate, and work on behalf of young children." This *all* includes adult learners. To support them, trainers need to identify and meet their needs.

NAEYC provides some ideas for meeting both goals. On its "Our Mission and Strategic Direction" page, it states: "We advocate for policies, practices, and systems that promote full and inclusive participation. We confront biases that create barriers and limit the potential of children, families, and early childhood professionals." In other words, systemic obstacles can interfere with someone's ability to function and thrive in the early childhood profession. The specific obstacles can vary, but many arise because a given early childhood professional's culture does not match the dominant culture in her area. By developing cultural responsiveness, trainers can better identify these challenges and work with adult learners to overcome them.

BECOMING CULTURALLY RESPONSIVE

So what do trainers actually do to become culturally responsive? The Center on Culture, Race, and Equity at the Bank Street College of Education employs a process called the Culturally Responsive Strength-Based (CRSB) Model Theory of Change to guide people along this path. The process includes three steps:

- **Personal:** Individuals examine their own beliefs and values. They identify any deficit-based attitudes and work to shift to an asset-based perspective. In other words, individuals examine negative perceptions about others and think of ways to see those perceptions in a positive light. If a person gives a frank response, a deficit-based attitude might declare her rude; an asset-based attitude values her honesty and forthrightness.

- **Professional:** Individuals build culturally responsive professional skills and practices. These could include cultivating cultural sensitivity by learning more about other cultures, listening to other viewpoints, and developing mutual respect for others.

- **Institutional:** The community works together to develop culturally relevant environments for children, families, and professionals. This requires community members to discuss how they can validate cultural identities and promote mutual respect within their community. This level includes making relevant systemic changes, such as establishing policies to reduce the barriers that culturally diverse families commonly face when accessing child care.

You can teach other early childhood professionals about cultural responsiveness through your example and by providing PL sessions on the topic. Consider how you can influence personal, professional, and institutional beliefs and values, and seek ways to turn deficit-based thinking into asset-based thoughts and actions.

Overcoming Biases

We all have biases. We often learn them within our own cultures or from our families and friends. They may also grow out of cultural differences. In many cases, we do not even realize that we have biases. Consider what biases you have about these topics:

- How to talk to children

- Gender identity

- Children's roles and responsibilities (how children should act and behave)

- Expected developmental milestones

- Discipline

- Diet and mealtime routines

- Toilet training

- Responses to crying

- Dress and hair care

- Sleep patterns and routines

- Messiness and cleanliness

Trainers need to be prepared to address participants' concerns about cultural and family differences. It is okay to have different opinions about how to care for and interact with children; however, all early childhood professionals, particularly trainers, need to prevent their biases from interfering with their work. We need to treat all adult learners fairly. Ask yourself, "Are there ways that I might discriminate against adult learners without realizing it?" For instance, might you assume that someone has little knowledge about a topic because she cannot articulate her thoughts in your primary language? Might you assume that someone does not understand the information presented because she looks distracted or refuses to participate? We all make assumptions—often incorrect ones—based on our perceptions. Take time to reflect on your assumptions about the adult learners you teach, and when you discover your unconscious biases, strive to develop asset-based perceptions of all adult learners.

LEARNING TO UNDERSTAND ADULT LEARNERS' CULTURES

As trainers work to become culturally responsive, they must build relationships and learn more about training participants. Trainers should seek to understand who adult learners are, what they think, and why they have certain ideas. To accomplish these goals, trainers need to be open and listen to learn about cultural differences.

One key part of this process is being sensitive to various expectations of what teachers and students should do in a learning environment. For instance, individuals raised in the West (North or South America or Western Europe) often have widely different values than individuals raised in the East (Asia or the Middle East). For example, according to Michael Michelini of Global from Asia, in Western cultures it is acceptable to think critically and debate with an instructor; in Eastern cultures, students are taught to submit to an instructor's authority and not question what is taught. As a more specific example, mainstream American culture believes that students should speak up if they do not understand, and then the teacher should reteach until the students do understand. But in some Asian cultures, the students' job is to respectfully listen and not ask questions (which would suggest that the teacher explained poorly, making her look bad). As a result, adult learners from these cultures might not ask for clarification even if they do not understand.

Obviously, trainers cannot learn about all cultural differences overnight and will make mistakes. But following certain practices will make the process smoother:

- Help adult learners from all cultures feel respected and accepted.

- Find out what learners already know and can do.

- Look for meaningful ways to allow all learners to share who they are and what they know.

More specifically, consider using some of the following strategies:

- Learn how to pronounce each adult learner's name correctly, and teach the pronunciation to the rest of the group. Ask each person to share what her name means and how it was chosen.

- Ask each learner to share one form of nonverbal communication that her culture deems important and to explain why it is important.

- Have learners from different cultures share how they communicate praise, displeasure, greetings, and so on.

- Give learners time to process information by having everyone think for a couple of minutes before you ask for responses. Some cultures value thinking deliberately and responding slowly after considering options.

- Use a variety of seating arrangements, and incorporate both individual and cooperative learning experiences.

Engagement Strategy: Me Museum

Try this activity to help participants from different cultures learn more about each other.

Materials

1 sheet of unlined paper per participant

pens or pencils

magazines

scissors

glue or tape

1. Give each person a piece of paper and set out the scissors, the glue or tape, and a variety of magazines.

2. Ask the participants to create collages for a Me Museum by either drawing pictures of things they like or cutting out pictures from the magazines and gluing or taping them onto their papers. Participants should not write their names on their papers. Once everyone has completed a collage, collect the papers.

3. Randomly pass the collages back out so that each participant has someone else's paper. Invite each person to look at the paper she received, think about what it represents, and write a short description of that collage's creator based on the pictures.

4. Ask for several volunteers to tell about the people whose papers they received. **Adaptation:** Invite class members to engage in a mixer to find out which collage belongs to each person. Participants can elaborate on why they selected different pictures for their pieces.

5. Post the collages on the wall to create a display. Invite the participants to enjoy a Me Museum viewing and discuss what they see in small groups. Later, you could add the creators' names to the papers.

LANGUAGE

Within a training session, you might have some participants who are still learning to understand and speak English. Try these ideas to promote a positive training experience for a linguistically diverse group:

- Use visuals, pictures, and videos. Turn on video subtitles if they are available.

- Incorporate small-group discussion and hands-on activities.

- Speak clearly, and if you must use acronyms or academic language, define what you mean in understandable terms. Look at body language and facial expressions to appraise whether someone understands what you say.

- Check in with adult learners periodically to see if they understand. For instance, ask participants to hold up their fingers to rate their understanding on a scale of one ("I am completely lost") to five ("I understand perfectly and am ready to move on").

- Find out what participants need to optimize learning. For example, when an early childhood teacher from Russia attended one of my training sessions, she asked to use her phone to translate words she did not know. This tool helped her understand most of what I said.

- After you explain a concept, have a participant restate the concept in her own words and give an example of what it would look in an early childhood classroom. (This strategy can help learners with all levels of English proficiency.)

- Allow more time than you think you need to for reading and writing activities.

- If the group includes bilingual participants, consider pairing them with English language learners. Even if the partners do not have the same native language, the bilingual person can empathize with and assist the English language learner.

- Provide one-on-one support.

- Be patient and respectful.

ABILITIES

Adult learners attending your training sessions may have physical or other types of disabilities. Some disabilities may be visible, but most of them will not be. The Americans with Disabilities Act (ADA; see the References section for a link to the full text of the law) requires that programs and trainers make reasonable accommodations and modifications for individuals with disabilities. *Reasonable* means that these adjustments should not place an undue burden on the program or the trainer. Here are some ideas for meeting common needs:

- **Visual challenges:** Use large print on visuals and handouts. Be careful about using colors that do not register correctly for someone who is color blind (such as reds, blues, and greens). Allow individuals to sit at the front of the meeting space if needed.

- **Hearing challenges:** Have a written script so participants with hearing impairments can follow along during training sessions. Speak clearly, and project your voice. Minimize secondary noise if possible; if not (for example, if the training space has a loud air-conditioning system that you cannot adjust), consider using a white-noise machine or app to mask unwanted sounds.

- **Sensory challenges:** Avoid extremes or sudden changes in your training environment's lighting, noise level, smells, textures, and sensory activities. Minimize distractions.

- **Mobility challenges:** Leave plenty of space among pieces of furniture when setting up. Keep electrical cords out of walking areas. If a participant cannot write or move easily or at all (for example, because of a wrist or leg injury), make modifications based on her specific needs.

One of the best ways to find out what an adult learner needs is to ask her. It may feel awkward, but the person will appreciate your desire to help her succeed. You can ask questions such as, "Do you prefer working individually or with a partner?" or "What types of activities best meet your needs?" You can help all learners by using a variety of learning strategies and presenting information in multiple formats. Be flexible and adaptive in creating an inclusive learning environment.

Trainers also need to recognize the challenges that some adult learners face as they become older. With age, most people face some cognitive decline. It may take them longer to recall information and express thoughts clearly. Age can hinder attention and the ability to multitask because it becomes harder for a person to keep multiple pieces of information in her mind at the same time. (Note that these same issues can appear when a person is stressed or has experienced a traumatic event, such as a death or another type of loss. For instance, after my mother passed away, I had difficulty thinking clearly as I went through the grieving process.) Other abilities that decline with age include mobility, reaction time, eyesight, hearing, taste, touch, and smell. Older adult learners may also resist learning new ideas or changing practices that have worked well for them over the years.

Despite these challenges, older adult learners have a wealth of life experiences that they can share, benefitting other adult learners with less experience. You can build on the strengths of older adult learners by involving them in discussions and problem solving. For example, during a training session on temperament that I attended, each participant received a unique paper doll that represented a child with certain temperament traits. The participants formed small groups to figure out the best strategies for meeting the needs of each child. Dione, an older participant, drew on her years of experience and offered multiple teaching strategies that had helped her meet the unique needs of real children. Some of the newer teachers especially appreciated Dione's insights.

CHAPTER 11:

Becoming an Effective Trainer

Zeki, a new trainer, has done plenty of research on his topic, written extensive notes, and created some discussion questions, so he feels ready for his first training session. He begins with a story about his teaching experiences, and the participants seem interested, but as he starts sharing all his research, people begin looking at their phones or putting their heads down. Zeki asks the group a question, and everyone stares blankly back at him. Beginning to panic, he starts talking again and somehow finishes the class.

Disheartened, Zeki meets with Antonio, an experienced trainer, for help. Antonio has Zeki do some self-reflection and complete a Trainer Reflection Tool for the training session. Zeki realizes that he needs to better understand adult learning principles and how to make his training more engaging. He accepts Antonio's invitation to attend some classes on becoming a more effective trainer.

Think about the best training session you have ever attended. Now think about the worst such session you have endured. As you ponder each experience, answer true or false for each statement:

- The trainer was prepared and knowledgeable.
- The trainer was engaging.
- The trainer made connections with the audience.
- The trainer shared stories related to the topic.
- The content was interesting and relevant.
- The participants had opportunities to discuss ideas.
- The participants engaged in a variety of learning activities.

How many statements were true for your best training experience? How about your worst training experience—were any of the statements true?

These statements illustrate important principles about what makes a trainer effective. This chapter uses a system called the Four Ps—plan, prepare, practice, and present—to teach you how to use those principles to become a confident and effective trainer.

PLAN

In many cases, you will create your own training materials and structure your own training sessions. But before you even create the first part of your presentation, you need a plan. This plan should include the training topic, the learning objectives, the engagement strategies you will use, the size of the group, the training space, and the unique needs of the learners.

Start your planning by asking yourself the following questions:

• Who are my learners?

• What topics are relevant to the needs of my learners?

• What objectives do I want to meet during my training session?

WHO ARE MY LEARNERS?

One key to being a confident and effective trainer is to know your audience. Who are the adult learners attending your training session? Why are they there? It would be great if trainers could say that all participants in their training sessions come because they want to learn about the topic. Unfortunately, some early childhood professionals attend training sessions only because they have to—for instance, because they need training hours for licensing. Your challenge is to create an environment and presentation that will draw all learners in and engage them in a dynamic learning experience. So start by finding out more about your learners:

• Collect information about learners on the registration form for your training session. For instance, you could ask learners to share where they work, their specific positions, and the ages of the children in their classrooms. Use this information to guide your preparation.

• Prior to the session, ask participants to complete a short electronic survey to assess their knowledge, understanding, and practices related to the training topic. For example, you could have participants fill out the first two sections of a KWL chart (see chapter 12). You can then print out the charts and return them to the participants at the end of the session so they can complete the final section.

• If you are not able to find out about participants ahead of time, use an engagement strategy at the beginning of the session to assess what they want to learn. See chapter 12 for some ideas.

WHAT TOPICS ARE RELEVANT TO THE NEEDS OF MY LEARNERS?

Observation and assessment data, if available, can help you identify training topics that matter to your learners. For example, when I was training teachers who were involved in a literacy initiative, their assessment data from the Early Language and Literacy Classroom Observation (ELLCO) informed my training planning and preparation. The data indicated that the majority of participating teachers rarely engaged in phonological-awareness activities with the children. The areas of emergent writing and extended conversations were also opportunities for growth. So as I planned my training sessions, I included information about these concepts, along with ideas about how the teachers could incorporate relevant activities into their classrooms.

If you do not have observational or assessment data, look at national, state, and community needs and trends to identify hot topics in early childhood. Pay attention to the topics being presented at state and national conferences. Also try talking to groups of early childhood professionals to learn more topics of interest.

Once you have chosen a topic, start researching it. The information you present should align with current research and evidence-based practices. Use scholarly resources, such as articles from early childhood journals, and access current information from government-sponsored websites and professional organizations, such as NAEYC and Zero to Three. Include references to state and national standards that relate to your topic (for instance, your state's pre-K science standards), and strive to connect your content to developmentally appropriate practices.

During your research, you will probably find more information than you can present. Limit the number of key points you present to avoid trying to cover too much. To home in on the most important concepts to cover, try using tools such as mind maps. You can also create a training outline that includes your objectives, main points, engagement strategies, and timing. (See appendix K for a sample training outline.)

Make sure the information you choose applies to real-life challenges that your learners face. Consider observing a variety of early childhood classrooms to learn what those challenges are and how you can make your material applicable to them. For example, activities that might work well in an infant classroom with two teachers and six infants might not be realistic for a classroom with two teachers and eight infants, including two infants with disabilities. Or if you are presenting a training session on science experiences, think about how you might need to adapt your strategies for, say, a classroom with twenty-five children and limited resources versus a classroom with fewer children and more resources.

WHAT OBJECTIVES DO I WANT TO MEET DURING MY TRAINING SESSION?

Take time to determine specific training objectives. An objective answers the question, "What do you want participants to be able to do at the end of the training session?" The objectives you create determine the type of training that you prepare. If you want participants to have greater awareness of a topic at the end of the training session, you should spend the majority of the session sharing content. If you want participants to gain new skills, you should spend most of the session helping participants process and practice those skills.

When creating objectives, use Bloom's Revised Taxonomy (as discussed by Lorin Anderson and David Krathwohl) as a guide. It describes six levels of cognition, each including related action verbs that can help you create objectives. The following list provides examples of the verbs and some sample objectives for each level:

- **Remember:** *recall, outline, identify, list*
  - Participants will be able to identify the five levels of Maslow's hierarchy of needs.
- **Understand:** *summarize, restate, describe, explain*
  - Participants will be able to summarize the main characteristics of developmentally appropriate practices.
- **Apply:** *predict, present, solve, demonstrate*
  - Participants will be able to demonstrate the correct steps of handwashing.
- **Analyze:** *examine, categorize, differentiate, contrast*
  - Participants will be able to contrast two different theories of child development.
- **Evaluate:** *critique, rank, recommend, rate*
  - Participants will be able to critique their lesson plans for meeting state standards.
- **Create:** *generate, invent, modify, design*
  - Participants will be able to design a preschool classroom following the principles of Universal Design for Learning.

PREPARE

Once you have determined your topic, your main points, and your objectives, you can begin preparing the training presentation. Take time to carefully arrange what you will say and do. Think through the logistics of implementing activities. Ensure all your materials are ready.

Here are some elements to consider as you prepare:

SLIDES AND SCRIPT

Many trainers use PowerPoints as part of their presentations. If you choose to do so, create slides that each feature applicable photos and a few key words. Use photos found on royalty-free source websites, such as pixabay.com and stocksnap.io. In the "notes" section of each slide (which you can see if you use presenter mode on your computer), write the main ideas you want to share. You can also print out these notes, bring them with you to the training session, and review them before presenting.

Some trainers prefer to write out the entire script for each presentation. This can be especially useful if you will be presenting the training session multiple times or if other trainers will also use your training session. You must individually determine how much written content you will need to present an effective training session.

ENGAGEMENT STRATEGIES

All learners benefit from multimodal instruction, or instruction with strategies that use multiple modalities (such as hearing, seeing, touching, and doing). Effective PL includes multimodal activities that reinforce the concepts taught. In this book, I use the term *engagement strategies* to refer to all methods for promoting multimodal instruction and involving participants in the learning process.

As you prepare your training sessions, determine the most appropriate engagement strategies based on the audience and the topic. See chapter 12 for a myriad of ideas.

Novelty often promotes engagement. Could you bring an interesting object to the training session to catch participants' interest? One trainer, for instance, arranged for several volunteers to wear different types of hats to represent various guidance approaches. The hats not only caught participants' interest but also became visual reminders of the concepts taught in the session. You could also show pictures of a novel object, see if the learners can guess what it is or what it does, and then explain how it relates to your training topic.

SHIFTS

Even with effective engagement strategies, most participants have limited attention spans. There is no standard agreement on the length of a person's attention span; however, it is hard for most adult learners to have sustained focus for long periods of time. Plan shifts, or changes in your instruction methods, at least every ten to twenty minutes to keep participants' minds and bodies alert. A shift could involve any of these activities:

- Ask participants a question and have them discuss it in pairs

- Show a video clip

- Ask participants to write responses on a flip chart or sticky note

- Have participants stand up and join a new group

- Engage participants in a brain break (see chapter 12)

HANDOUTS

To have or not to have handouts? That is the question. If you decide to use them, handouts should enhance and reinforce content. Some trainers love to create extensive packets, and other trainers do not use any handouts. When making this decision, think about factors such as the training topic, your objectives, and the audience.

Consider sharing handouts electronically. You might email the handouts to participants or create a webpage where they can access them. In one training session I attended, the trainer posted a scan code on the PowerPoint, and the participants used reader apps to access the handouts. This is a great way to share handouts if your audience has the tools and technical abilities to use a scan code.

MAKE AND TAKE

Teachers appreciate being able to make something that they can immediately use in their classrooms. If you use this technique in a training session, the product should correspond with the training topic. Meaningful make-and-takes include felt finger puppets, simple musical instruments, and literacy props. As you assemble the materials for the make-and-take, include activity cards with instructions on how to use the finished items in the classroom.

PLAN FOR THE UNEXPECTED

Ironically, part of your planning should include plans for things that you do not expect to actually happen. Let me illustrate with an experience of my own.

Years ago, I was in a large room in a conference center, presenting to about four hundred people. As I was showing a video clip, both of the room's large screens went blank. The whole audiovisual (A/V) system had shut down. I had a short moment of panic. Now what?

Fortunately, I had created plans for just this kind of situation. While the room monitor ran to find the conference center's A/V person, I reviewed my options and decided to hold a question-and-answer session until the system was back up. Because it was such a large group, I took the microphone and started going around the room answering questions. Within about fifteen minutes, the A/V person arrived and fixed the system, and I was able to show the rest of the video and finish my planned presentation.

Another time, my laptop froze during a presentation. This time, I reverted to a different backup plan and had participants talk to a partner about our training topic while I rebooted my laptop. Most participants are very sympathetic to what I call *training trauma*, but you still do not want them to have to wait very long without something to do.

As these stories show, even with excellent preparation, sooner or later you will have a mishap during a training session. What will you do if your computer freezes, your video will not play, or your PowerPoint will not advance? if the electricity goes out and you are in a room without windows? if you finish early or realize that you cannot cover all your content? The answer to all these questions is to have a plan and be prepared. Here are some ideas for backup plans:

- Have small groups or partners discuss a thought question.

- Conduct a question-and-answer session.

- Have participants complete a planned backup activity related to your topic.

- Go on with the presentation without your PowerPoint (make sure to bring a printed copy so you have something to follow).

PRACTICE

Practice, practice, practice. Did I say practice?

To become a confident and effective trainer, you need to practice not just your specific presentation but also your general presentation skills. Think about your tone of voice, body language, and eye contact. Think of multiple ways to ask and answer questions. One trainer I knew created notes to herself at different points within her presentation as reminders to smile, slow down, take a deep breath, and have fun!

Practicing helps you determine the pacing and timing of your presentation. It is also a good time to check out the technology you plan to use. It is important to spend sufficient time practicing your presentation. Try the following strategies:

- Practice your training presentation on a small group of family and friends (or inanimate objects). Try out different engagement strategies. Practice making eye contact. Determine what works and what you need to revise.

- Practice different ways to add novelty and interest to your presentation, such as telling stories or humorous anecdotes.

- Consider videotaping yourself. As you watch the video, assess your tone, inflection, gestures, body language, eye contact, and idiosyncrasies (such as frequently saying "um" or "okay").

- Practice does not always need to involve standing up and presenting your entire training session. The key is to find the practice method that works best for you. Some trainers, for example, practice using visualization, or thinking through their presentations step by step and imagining clearly what they will need and do. By giving you the chance to practice your training session without using your PowerPoint or physical materials, this technique allows you to focus on what to say and how to say it.

PRESENT

You have spent sufficient time planning, preparing, and practicing. Now it is time to present. As you get ready to present, dress professionally, selecting clothes that have a pop of color and interesting features. And always remember to wear a smile!

SET UP THE ENVIRONMENT

Arrive at least thirty to sixty minutes prior to your start time to allow yourself sufficient time to set up. Strive to have everything ready to go at least twenty minutes before start time. This gives you cushion time to make adjustments if something does not go as planned, and it gives you the opportunity to interact with participants as they arrive.

- **Arrange the room:** Arrange the furniture in a way that will promote the desired level of interaction. For sessions with less interaction, arrange tables and chairs in theater or classroom style, in which rows of chairs face the front of the room. For sessions with more interaction, arrange tables and chairs in a U, a circle, or small clusters. Make sure to leave enough space among pieces of furniture so that any participants with mobility devices (wheelchairs, crutches, and so on) can get around safely.

- **Add visual interest:** Add elements to the room that will soften the environment and provide interesting things to look at. Here are some examples:

  - Place bright fabric or scarves in the middle of each table. Add battery-operated tea lights.

  - Scatter fall leaves, red hearts, or other seasonal items around the room.

  - Add colorful placemats to the center of each table. Place handouts and activity props underneath the placemats to keep them hidden until needed.

  - Use colorful containers to hold markers, pens, sticky notes, and fidgets for participants to use. Fidgets are items that participants can manipulate, such as pipe cleaners, playdough, stress balls, and toys. Learners who like to keep their hands busy love fidgets!

  - Post pictures and quotes related to the training topic around the room.

- **Make it comfortable:** Create a comfortable and emotionally safe environment for yourself and your participants. Your words and actions promote emotional security. As mentioned in chapter 2, you can create climate-of-care guidelines with participants to establish norms for interaction. If you feel comfortable, your participants are more likely to feel comfortable, too.

START BY MAKING CONNECTIONS

Before the training session begins, start to make connections with participants. This will begin the process of creating an emotionally safe environment and help put participants at ease.

- Welcome participants at the door.

- Talk to participants after they have settled into their seats.

- Introduce yourself to people you have not met before.

- Greet people by name if you already know them.

- Ask questions to learn more about your audience members.

USE TIME WISELY

It can be tempting to wait until everyone arrives before starting, especially if you are training a small group. However, respect the individuals who arrived promptly by starting and ending on time (or a few minutes earlier).

Plan to have breaks during your session. I have found that participants have more energy if they have more-frequent breaks—five to seven minutes every hour works well. Break time gives everyone a chance to stand up and move, check their phones, go to the restroom, and talk with other learners. To help participants be more mindful of the time, state exactly when you want them to return from a break. For example, you might say, "Please return at 6:45 p.m." Use a PowerPoint slide with a timer that counts down the time. This tool can help everyone (including you) know when to begin wrapping up break activities. Be sure to pace yourself during your presentation so that you can cover all of your main points.

PRESENTATION TECHNIQUES

Just prior to beginning the training session, prepare yourself to be calm, relaxed, and confident. Use positive self-talk. Breathe deeply to relax your mind and body. Smile—and begin!

During your presentation, ask clear questions. Try giving participants sample answers to provide a frame of reference for the type of answers you are seeking. This technique helps learners think of their own ideas and examples.

Give participants time to think about what to share. If you feel uncomfortable with silence, focus on counting down from ten to one slowly before speaking again. Tell the group, "I'm going to give you some time to think about your answers before taking responses." This strategy benefits individuals who need more time to process questions and formulate responses.

During your presentation, watch for adult learners' cues. What nonverbal signals are you seeing? Look at participants' eyes and facial expressions. Are learners watching you (suggesting that they are interested in the topic), or are they looking off in the distance or giving you blank stares when you ask a question (suggesting that they are disengaged)? What is the overall mood of the room?

It can be particularly tricky to transition adult learners from small-group activities back to whole-group activities. Consider using these strategies:

- Listen for the level of voice volume. When the voice volume lowers, it signals that participants are finishing their conversations.

- Give small groups a one-minute warning to wrap up their conversations.

- Use a noisemaker or another type of attention-getter to bring the large group back together.

Pay attention to your body language and gestures. When asking participants to respond to a question, avoid pointing directly at someone; this gesture can be considered rude. Instead, look and nod at the person or use your hand, palm up, to gesture toward him. Make and maintain eye contact with participants throughout the training session, and smile!

Adult learners generally welcome and enjoy good humor. If chosen and presented carefully, fun stories, anecdotes, and videos can lift participants' spirits and enhance the training experience. Humor can also ease the tension if something goes wrong during the session. For instance, if your A/V system fails, you could make a joke about leaving everyone in the dark about the topic. These types of comments can ease the tension and stress you and the participants may be feeling after a mishap.

Be professional and enthusiastic as you present. Use respectful words and actions. People respond positively to positive energy, so your enthusiasm for your topic can be contagious.

USING THE TRAINER REFLECTION TOOL

The Trainer Reflection Tool (TRT), available in appendix L, can help trainers reflect on their training sessions and can help supervisors provide feedback to trainers. The TRT has three main sections:

- **Create a Climate of Caring Connections:** Evaluates whether the trainer built an environment in which learners felt safe and connected

- **Present a Prepared and Effective Presentation:** Evaluates whether the trainer was prepared and used strategies that helped participants meet the learning objectives

- **Implement Adult Learning Principles:** Evaluates how well the trainer followed the six adult learning principles described in chapter 9

Each section includes several related practices. The person completing the form rates each practice depending on the level at which the trainer implemented it (high, mid, or low). There is also space to list glows and grows.

The TRT helps trainers identify what they are doing well and areas for growth. The supervisor completes the tool while observing a training presentation. The trainer completes the tool after the session. Then, similar to the coaching conversations described in chapter 8, the trainer and the supervisor meet and discuss their results. When trainers and supervisors use this tool, trainers can strengthen their presentations to help them meet these goals:

- More effectively engage adult learners

- Implement adult learning principles

- Build connections

CHAPTER 12:

Engagement Strategies

When Hailey, a preschool teacher, arrives at tonight's training session, the trainer greets her warmly. The session begins with an engaging icebreaker. The trainer introduces some positive-guidance strategies and shows several video clips to demonstrate the strategies. Then the participants form small groups, identify challenges they face, and discuss solutions. Throughout the session, these and similar learning activities help Hailey internalize the concepts. She leaves refreshed and excited to implement what she has learned.

Effective engagement strategies include a wide variety of methods that trainers use to keep learners interested and involved in the topic. During engagement strategies, learners are actively involved in processing and retaining information, so the strategies reinforce the main concepts being taught. Learners benefit when they can hear, see, discuss, and experience learning material in a variety of ways. The ideas in this chapter are some of my favorites from my many years of facilitating professional learning.

WHICH STRATEGIES SHOULD I USE?

When selecting an engagement strategy, begin by identifying what you want to accomplish. Are you trying to:

- obtain the learners' attention?

- give the learners a brain break (which we define later in this chapter)?

- promote interaction by placing learners in different groups?

- build connections among learners?

- give learners opportunities to share and learn from each other?

- engage learners in reflection?

- give learners opportunities to review content?

Adult learners benefit from all seven of these types of engagement strategies. Whichever strategies you choose, remember to make them meaningful and connect them to the training content.

ATTENTION-GETTERS

During a given training session, you will need to gain or regain the group's attention multiple times. Noisemakers work well for this purpose. My favorite noisemaker is bells on a stick—they make a pleasant noise and quickly gain participants' attention. Other possible instruments include a simple xylophone, a gong, or wind chimes. Also consider using these other types of attention-getters:

- Hold up three fingers and slowly count down: "Three, two, one." After *one*, resume your presentation.

- Say, "If you can hear me, touch your nose. If you can hear me, pat your head. If you can hear me, clap three times." You can substitute any type of action in your directions, and generally you will have the participants' attention by the fourth command.

- Ask participants to give you a thumbs-up (or some other positive gesture in your culture) to show that they are ready.

- Tell participants, "Wrap it up." Wait a moment, and then say, "Finish up your last sentence." Pause, and then say slowly in a deep voice, "Speak your last word" (this really gets everyone's attention).

- Tell everyone to give you a drumroll in preparation for the next topic.

- Use a call-and-response phrase. At the beginning of the training session, explain to the adult learners that when you say a certain word or phrase, they should respond with a different word or phrase. For example, tell the group, "When I say *positive*, you say *guidance*," or "When I say *macaroni and cheese*, you say *everybody freeze*." Be creative! Practice with the whole group a few times, and then use the phrase throughout the session. You might have to repeat the call several times to get everyone's attention.

BUILDING CONNECTIONS: RELATIONSHIPS, RELATIONSHIPS, RELATIONSHIPS

When I talk to teachers about caring for children, I emphasize relationships, relationships, relationships. Likewise, positive relationships among adult learners affect their learning and development. You can help build those connections by creating an emotionally safe environment that allows participants to feel comfortable participating and sharing their thoughts.

WARM-UP CONNECTORS

The trainer sets the tone for a training session from the first moment the adult learners enter the room. You begin building connections as you welcome participants. When you begin the actual training session, continue that building process by starting off with some type of icebreaker or, as I prefer to call it, warm-up connector.

Warm-Up Connector: Five Fun Facts

This activity helps participants learn more about the trainer and each other. This learning causes adult learners to begin to feel connected.

1. Prior to the training session, create a PowerPoint slide with pictures that represent five fun facts about yourself. These facts could include favorites (foods, colors, vacation spots, and so on), pets, hobbies, talents, or unique experiences or traditions (such as marrying one's high school sweetheart or having a family tradition of making tamales for holidays).

2. At the beginning of the session, share your five fun facts with the group.

3. Instruct participants to pair up and share five fun facts about themselves.

4. Ask a few people to share fun facts about themselves with the whole group.

For example, here are five fun facts about me:

• My favorite color is purple.

• My favorite flower is the iris (especially purple irises!).

• My family and I have three pet birds: two cockatiels named Max and Charlotte and one parakeet named Venus.

• My favorite artist is Monet, and I love his paintings that include water lilies and a Japanese bridge.

• I was born on Christmas Eve. Instead of being delivered by the stork, I was delivered by Santa Claus. I even came home from the hospital in a red Christmas stocking.

You can make some interesting connections by sharing fun facts. I love meeting other people who enjoy purple irises and Monet's paintings. My favorite connection experience happened at a training session I did in California—a participant came up to me afterwards and said, "My name is also Teresa, I was born on December 22, and I came home from the hospital in a red Christmas stocking!" Now that's a connection!

Warm-Up Connector: Like Me

This quick and easy activity can help trainers learn about participants.

1. Prior to the training session, create a list of statements designed to build connections. The statements can be related to the training topic or just for fun.

2. During the training session, call out one statement at a time. Ask those to whom a statement applies to stand up and look around. **Adaptation:** Have participants form a circle facing each other and step forward if a statement is true for them. This method works well with smaller groups, as participants can quickly see who is "like me."

3. For some of the statements, ask participants to share additional information (see examples below).

Try some of these statements:

- Stand up if you have been in early childhood education for less than two years.

- Stand up if you have been in early childhood education for two to ten years.

- Stand up if you have been in early childhood education for more than ten years. (After this statement, find out who has worked in this field the longest.)

- Stand up if you were born outside of the United States. (Ask participants who stand up to share where they were born.)

- Stand up if you have lived in Nevada (or whatever state you are in) your entire life.

- Stand up if you are left-handed.

- Stand up if your favorite children's book is *Brown Bear, Brown Bear, What Do You See?* (This statement works well for a training session on literacy.)

- Stand up if you enjoy messy art projects.

- Stand up if you like dogs more than cats.

- Stand up if you love sitting on the beach and watching the sun set.

Try to craft statements that will build connections among your particular group of participants. People tend to seek out others who are like them during breaks and talk about common interests.

Warm-Up Connector: Phone Photos

Most participants will probably have cell phones that include photos. In my experience, this activity always generates high energy and excitement.

1. Before the training session, create a PowerPoint slide with a photo from your phone that represents something you enjoy doing. **Adaptation:** Alternatively, you could use the last photo you took, a photo that represents early childhood education, or a photo that fits into a certain category (such as your funniest photo, your cutest photo, or a vacation photo).

2. During the training session, show the slide and explain how the photo relates to the topic or category you chose. For example, you could share a photo of a sunset and talk about how you love watching the brilliant colors as the sun sets.

3. Ask each participant to select a photo from her own phone that fits the specified topic or category.

4. Direct participants to pair up, share their photos with each other, and explain how their photos fit the topic or category.

5. **Extension:** If you will be having a future training session with the same group, ask participants to take photos that relate to the next training topic. For example, if the next session will focus on dramatic play, instruct participants to bring pictures of their dramatic-play areas. Specify some categories of photos to take, such as participants' most interesting dramatic-play props and favorite dramatic-play outfits. At the next training session, have participants share their photos and learn more about the dramatic-play centers at each other's programs.

Warm-Up Connector: "Would You Rather . . . ?"

This activity helps participants make connections with each other and with the training topic.

1. Before the training session, create several "Would you rather . . . ?" questions that relate to the training topic. It may help to write the questions on a PowerPoint slide so participants can read them.

2. During the session, present one statement at a time.

3. After each statement, have every participant find a new partner and share why she selected one choice over the other.

Here are some ideas for training topics and corresponding "Would you rather . . . ?" questions:

Training Topics	"Would You Rather . . . ?" Questions
Outdoor play Sensory issues	Would you rather walk barefoot or wear shoes? Why?
Process art Fine motor skills	Would you rather create a messy art project or put together a puzzle? Why?
Children with disabilities	Would you rather lose the ability to read or lose the ability to speak? Why?

Warm-Up Connector: Pack Your Worries

When adult learners enter a training room, they often bring along some concerns. They may be worried about their families, children from their classrooms, or other responsibilities and tasks that they need to complete. To help participants symbolically set their worries aside, try this exercise. The act of writing down concerns helps to release them from the conscious mind so that participants can shift their focus to the training topic.

1. Give each person a piece of paper with a simple outline of a backpack.

2. Instruct participants to write down all their current concerns on their backpacks.

3. Have participants then tape their papers to the wall in the back of the room, with the images facing the wall so that no one can see them.

4. Ask the group to set aside their worries until the end of the training session. Assure them that they can pick up their backpacks at the end of the session, or they can leave them behind.

Warm-Up Connector: It's in the Bag

The creativity of some groups really shines during this activity.

1. At the beginning of the training session, ask each participant to take something out of her bag or purse that illustrates her approach to teaching children.

2. Invite several participants to show and explain their items.

For example, in one training session I attended, a teacher took out some knitting needles and yarn. She described how she strives to "knit" the children in her class together by using the right "stitches" (strategies) and paying attention so that she does not "drop a stitch" (miss children's cues).

Adaptation: Turn this exercise into a team-building game by splitting participants into small groups and asking them to search their bags or purses for a certain number of items that fit into specific categories. For example, assign each team to find four things: something they could use to teach children; something they could use to decorate a classroom; something they could read to children; and something they could use to play with children.

Warm-Up Connector: Name Poems

This activity works well when you have a larger group of individuals who do not know each other.

Materials

1 sheet of lined paper per participant

pens or pencils

1 sheet of flip-chart paper for every 6 participants

markers

1. Before the training session, make a PowerPoint slide with these four questions:

   • Where did your first name come from? (For example, you might be named after a family member, or your parents might have liked a certain name.)

   • Who gave you your name?

   • Do you like your name? Why or why not?

   • Were you ever teased about your name?

2. During the training session, give each person a piece of paper (and a pen or pencil, if needed). Display the slide, and have participants write down their answers to the questions.

3. Tell everyone to find a partner whom she does not know. Give the pairs about one minute to share their answers.

4. Instruct each partnership to pair up with two other partnerships and form a group of six. Have each person share information on her partner's name with the other group members.

5. Pass out a sheet of flip-chart paper and markers to each group of six. Direct each group to create a name poem by writing down all group members' names and some information related to each name.

6. When all the poems are finished, invite each group to come to the front of the room and read their poem. Encourage each group member to wave when her name is spoken in the poem.

Here is an example of one group's name poem and the explanations for each line:

Elizabeth the queen. (She was named after Queen Elizabeth.)

Jasmine the flower. (Her mother liked jasmine flowers.)

Tapika from Kansas? (She was named for the state capital of Kansas, but her name is spelled differently.)

Mary had a little lamb. (She was teased with this rhyme as a child.)

They all got into Shronda's Honda. (Her name was often mispronounced.)

Sayonara! (Her name means "goodbye" in Japanese.)

ANYTIME CONNECTORS

As trainers, we want adult learners to connect to each other throughout training sessions, not just at the beginning. Try some of these activities to build connections during other parts of a training session.

Anytime Connector: Making a Connection

1. Have everyone, including you, form a circle.

2. Starting with you and moving clockwise, ask each person to share a word or phrase related to the word *connection*. Encourage every participant to share something unique.

3. When everyone has shared, split the participants into groups of three.

4. Instruct the groups to discuss how they can make connections with the children they teach in their classrooms.

For example, you could start by saying, "When I think of the word *connection*, I think about relationships." The next three participants might share the words *empathy*, *partnership*, and *belonging*.

Anytime Connector: Minute-to-Win-It Games

In Minute-to-Win-It games, participants have one minute to complete a challenge either as individuals or as a team. These activities make great team-building exercises. Try searching online for a countdown timer with music and adding it to your PowerPoint slides. After the game, lead a whole-group discussion on topics such as teamwork and communication.

Here are two of my favorite Minute-to-Win-It challenges (you can find more online):

Stacking Cups

In this challenge, the goal is to create the tallest tower in one minute. Towers often fall before time runs out, leaving teams scrambling to build them back up. The tallest tower is frequently over twelve cups high.

Materials

16 plastic cups per team

16 index cards (4″ x 6″) per team

1. Place participants in teams of four to six people.

2. Give each team a set of cups and index cards.

3. Tell the teams that they must create the tallest tower possible in one minute by alternating cups and index cards.

4. Start the timer, and watch the fun!

5. When time runs out, count the cups and cards in each tower to find the tallest one. Lead a round of applause for the winners.

Creating Pyramids

Teams attempt to create a pyramid in less than one minute. Teams can often complete this challenge before time runs out.

Materials

6 plastic cups per team

rubber band with 6 long strings attached to it at equal increments (1 set per team)

1. Place participants in teams of six members, and pass out the materials.

2. Explain that each team member must hold the end of a string and pull or relax to adjust the rubber band.

3. Announce that the teams have one minute to build a pyramid (three cups on the bottom, two cups in the middle, and one cup at the top) without touching the cups with their hands.

4. Start the timer, and watch the fun!

5. When time runs out, lead a round of applause for all teams that completed their pyramids.

Anytime Connector: Commonalities and Uniqueness

This activity helps participants learn about their shared and unique characteristics or experiences.

1. Split participants into teams of four to six members. **Adaptation:** Have participants complete this activity in pairs.

2. Instruct each team to find out five experiences or characteristics that are the same for everyone on the team. Invite each team to share with the large group and see if any of the team's commonalities also apply to others in the large group. For example, a team might share that all its members are preschool teachers, were born in the United States, have pets, have children, and love ice cream.

3. Now ask the teams to find out something unique about each team member. Invite the teams to share with the large group anything that they think might also be unique within the large group.

4. To continue the previous example, this team might share that only Tina has traveled to Australia, only Latosha has a pet hamster, only Emily water-skis, only Keisha has four children, and only Rachel was born on the Fourth of July.

Anytime Connector: One-Minute Listen

This activity demonstrates the importance of active listening with peers, children, and family members.

1. Ask each person to find a partner.

2. Present a topic. Explain that Partner A will talk to Partner B about that topic for one minute. Partner B must actively listen and only respond nonverbally (such as by nodding and smiling).

3. Start the timer.

4. When time runs out, present a new topic. Explain that the partners will now switch roles, with Partner B talking to Partner A about the new topic.

5. Start the timer again.

6. When time runs out, ask participants to share how it felt to be the talker and the listener. Consider also asking the group the following discussion questions:

   • Did not being able to respond verbally make a difference in how you listened?

   • Was it hard to only listen?

   • How did it feel to talk and receive only nonverbal feedback?

   • Did you feel that the other person was actively listening?

GROUPING TECHNIQUES

Adult learners benefit from interacting with a variety of participants. You can facilitate this behavior by using a variety of grouping techniques throughout a training session. Here are five of my favorite grouping techniques.

GROUPING TECHNIQUE: CLOCK PARTNERS

This activity provides a quick and effective way to match participants with different partners throughout your training session.

Materials

1 copy of "Clock Partners" handout per participant (see appendix M)

pens or pencils

1. Give everyone a copy of the "Clock Partners" handout (and a pen or pencil, if needed).

2. Tell the participants that they each need to find four different partners, preferably people they do not already know, and make appointments to meet later in the training session. When a person finds her first partner, she writes that person's name on her own paper by one of the times (such as 12 o'clock). She repeats this process until she has found a total of four different partners. Tip: If you have an uneven number of participants, there can be one group of three for each time slot.

3. Throughout the training session, have participants meet with each of their clock partners. For example, ask 3 o'clock partners to discuss a question. Later, tell 6 o'clock partners to share examples of how they have applied a teaching strategy in their classrooms. Use other activities to have participants work with their 9 o'clock and 12 o'clock partners sometime during the session.

GROUPING TECHNIQUE: NUMBER, COLOR, SHAPE

This technique enables you to quickly form groups at three different times during a training session.

Materials

1 index card per participant

markers

1. Prior to the training session, write a number on one side of each index card and draw a colored shape on the other side. For example, if you wanted to have six groups during each group-time segment, you could use the numbers one through six; the colors red, blue, green, orange, purple, and pink; and the shapes circle, square, triangle, rectangle, diamond, and star. Mix up the numbers, colors, and shapes on the different cards so that each card is unique. **Tip:** You can increase or decrease the number of groups by using more or fewer numbers, colors, and shapes.

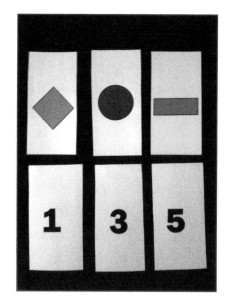

2. At the beginning of the training session, give each participant a card. Instruct everyone to keep her card throughout the session.

3. During the session, ask participants to form groups based on the numbers on their cards.

4. Later, instruct participants to form groups based on the colors on their cards.

5. Finally, direct the participants to form groups based on the shapes on their cards.

GROUPING TECHNIQUE: SILENT LINE-UP

The dynamics of a group really change when participants are instructed not to talk. Participants get quite creative as they try to communicate without speaking. This activity serves as both an engagement strategy and a grouping technique.

1. Using only nonverbal communication, direct participants to line up in chronological order by their birthdays without talking.

2. Once everyone is lined up, ask each person to state her birthday. If people are out of order, have them adjust accordingly.

3. When the line is in the correct order, invite each participant to pair up with a person next to her and discuss a topic such as nonverbal communication.

GROUPING TECHNIQUE: SALTY, SWEET, SPICY, OR MILD
Materials

4 sheets of flip-chart paper

markers

1. Prior to the training session, post four sheets of flip-chart paper in different areas of the room. Write a different title ("Salty," "Sweet, "Spicy," or "Mild") on each paper.

2. Ask participants to select whether they prefer salty, sweet, spicy, or mild food. Explain that this is a forced-choice question, so they can select only one option.

3. Direct all participants with the same answer to form a group by the corresponding paper, resulting in up to four groups total.

4. Give each group markers, and have the groups discuss a topic, such as food allergies in the classroom or sensory preferences. Ask each group to write the main ideas from their discussions on their charts.

5. Invite the groups to share their main points with the large group.

GROUPING TECHNIQUE: SOLE MATE

This activity offers a fun way to have participants find learning partners.

1. Invite each participant to find her "sole mate," or someone who has the same (or close to the same) shoe size. **Adaptation:** Suggest that each participant find a partner who is the same (or close to the same) height, has the same birthday month or season, works with the same age group of children, has worked in the early childhood field for (approximately) the same amount of time, or has the same birth order in her family (oldest, middle, youngest, or only child).

2. Have participants go around the room comparing shoe sizes (or whatever characteristic you choose) until each person finds a (close) match.

3. Ask the partners to discuss a question related to the training topic.

GROUPING TECHNIQUE: PIECE THE PUZZLE

This activity serves as both a grouping technique and an engagement strategy.

Materials

1 puzzle with interlocking pieces for every 4 participants

1. Prior to the training session, create your puzzles. Each puzzle should have four pieces that form a picture on one side; on the other side, each piece should have a quotation or question. You can use the same text for each puzzle if you want all groups to discuss the same topic, or you can use a different text for each group.

2. During the training session, randomly give each participant a puzzle piece.

3. Ask the participants to form groups by finding the people with the corresponding pieces.

4. Direct each group to read and discuss the quotations or questions on their puzzle pieces.

READING ENGAGEMENT STRATEGIES

These strategies promote meaningful discussions about reading assignments.

READING ENGAGEMENT STRATEGY: TWO CLICKS AND ONE CLUNK

Use this activity when you will have multiple training sessions with the same group and a reading assignment in between. This strategy gives reading assignments more meaning because group members know they will have time to discuss their ideas, pose questions, and clarify topics.

1. When giving the reading assignment, ask each participant to write down two "clicks" (two things that resonate with her) and one "clunk" (an idea that did not resonate with her or that she has questions about) from the reading. Remind participants to bring their clicks and clunks to the next session for discussion.

2. At the next session, place participants in small groups, and instruct them to discuss their clicks and clunks.

3. Invite a few participants to share their clicks and clunks with the large group.

READING ENGAGEMENT STRATEGY: 3, 2, 1

Use this strategy for PL experiences with multiple sessions.

Materials

1 copy of "3, 2, 1" handout per participant (see appendix N)

1. When giving the reading assignment, pass out the "3, 2, 1" handout, and ask participants to complete it in connection with their reading.

2. At the beginning of the next session, have participants form small groups, and invite them to share and discuss their ideas and questions.

READING ENGAGEMENT STRATEGY: TWO RECALLS AND TWO INSIGHTS

Use this strategy for PL experiences with multiple sessions.

Materials

4 sheets of flip-chart paper (or more if your group is large)

markers

1. Before the training session, post four sheets of flip-chart paper on the walls. Title the charts "Recalls and Insights." Leave the markers near the charts.

2. As participants enter the room, ask each person to write down two recalls and two insights from her reading on one of the charts.

3. Divide participants into four small groups. Have each group go to one of the charts and discuss what is written on the chart and how it relates to their own recalls and insights.

4. Invite each small group to share several key ideas with the large group.

READING ENGAGEMENT STRATEGY: READ AND MARK

Use this strategy when participants will complete a reading assignment during a training session. This strategy facilitates more engagement with reading materials and promotes richer discussions about the reading.

Materials

1 copy of the reading assignment per participant

small sticky notes

pens or pencils

1. Before the training session, create a PowerPoint slide explaining three symbols that participants will use to mark their reading assignments. You can use whatever symbols you choose. The following list provides an example:

- A check mark to mean, "I understand this concept."

- A smiley face to mean, "I think I know what this is, but I would like to learn more about it."

- A question mark to mean, "What is this?"

2. During the session, give each person some small sticky notes (and a pen or pencil, if needed).

3. Instruct participants to mark their assignments as they read by drawing the symbols on the sticky notes and placing them near the applicable text.

4. Once everyone finishes reading and marking, split participants into small groups. Invite them to share the items that they understood and to discuss their questions and the topics they want to learn more about.

SHARING AND LEARNING ENGAGEMENT STRATEGIES

Adult learners value learning from each other. Try these strategies to involve participants in this important process.

SHARING AND LEARNING ENGAGEMENT STRATEGY: PASSWORD TRIANGLE

This is one of my favorite strategies for introducing a new topic.

1. Prior to the training session, create a PowerPoint slide that includes a triangle divided into four sections. In each section, write one word related to the topic. Animate the words on the slide so that one new word will appear each time you advance the presentation.

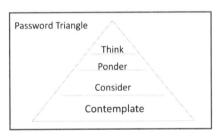

2. During the session, ask everyone to find a partner and to designate one person as Partner A and the other person as Partner B.

3. Explain that the group will be playing a game called Password Triangle. As in the game show Password, one partner will give verbal or nonverbal clues about a password while the other partner tries to guess the word. When the guessing partner says the correct word, the partners should high-five, switch places, and wait for the next word. As there are four passwords, each person will give clues for two words and try to guess two words.

4. Instruct Partner A to face the screen and Partner B to put her back to the screen.

5. Post the first password on the screen. Direct Partner A to begin giving clues and Partner B to try to guess the word. If Partner B guesses the word, remind the partners to high-five and switch places.

6. When most of the participants have guessed the password, use a noisemaker to get the group's attention. Tell the still-guessing pairs to have the partners switch places, even if the guesser hasn't figured out the word yet.

7. Repeat this process for the three remaining passwords.

8. Thank participants for playing. Invite them to return to their seats, and then lead a whole-group discussion about the four passwords and how they relate to the main topic.

Here are some sample topics and password triangles:

- For a discussion on reflection, use the passwords *think, ponder, consider, and contemplate.*

- For a discussion on the quality of feedback, use the passwords *assistance, hints, information, and encouragement.*

- For a discussion on positive guidance, use the passwords *coach, support, teach,* and *calm.*

SHARING AND LEARNING ENGAGEMENT STRATEGY: MIX AND MINGLE

This strategy allows learners to move around the room and talk to different partners about specific statements or questions.

1. Before the training session, create a PowerPoint slide with statements or questions. Select a short, upbeat instrumental music track to play during the mix-and-mingle segments.

2. At the appropriate time in the session, post the slide. Ask each person to silently read the statements or questions and select two that she would like to discuss.

3. Tell the participants to mix and mingle, as if at a social gathering, while the music is playing. Start the music.

4. When the music stops, instruct everyone to find a partner and discuss the first statement or question that each person selected, including why she picked it.

5. Start the music again, and encourage participants to mix and mingle again.

6. When the music stops, have each person find a different partner and talk about the second statement or question that each person selected, including why she chose it.

7. Start the music a third time, and instruct participants to mix and mingle back to their seats.

SHARING AND LEARNING ENGAGEMENT STRATEGY: ROUND ROBIN

This strategy allows adult learners to share, categorize, and prioritize ideas.

Materials

5 sheets of flip-chart paper

pens or pencils

sticky notes

10 colored dot stickers per participant

1. Prior to the training session, post the sheets of flip-chart paper around the room and title each chart with an element of an early childhood classroom: "Activities," "Interactions," "Materials," "Environment," and "Routines."

2. During the training session, hand out sticky notes (and a pen or pencil, if needed) to participants.

3. Ask participants to write ideas on the sticky notes about how each element relates to the training topic. Explain that they can write multiple sticky notes for each element.

4. Request that participants post their sticky notes on the corresponding charts.

5. Split participants into five groups, and send one group to each chart.

6. Instruct the groups to read through the sticky notes, categorize them by moving them into groups of similar ideas, and label each category.

7. Give every participant ten dot stickers.

8. Have participants go around and read all the charts. Direct each person to select what she considers the two main or most important ideas on each chart and to place a sticker next to each.

9. Identify the ideas with the most stickers, and lead a whole-group discussion about those ideas.

Any topic that has multiple dimensions can work with this strategy. For example, if you are training participants on promoting language development in young children, you could ask participants to write down ideas of how each element on the charts relates to language development. For the "Activities" chart, participants might write "singing songs" and "reading books" as ideas that promote language development.

SHARING AND LEARNING ENGAGEMENT STRATEGY: KWL CHART

Use this strategy to find out what your participants already know about a subject, what questions they have, and what misconceptions they might have brought to the training session. Later, finish the activity by having participants fill in what they have learned.

Materials

1 sheet of flip-chart paper per group

markers

1. Prior to the training session, create a KWL chart for each group by writing the training topic at the top of a sheet of flip-chart paper and dividing the rest of the paper into three sections. Label the top section "Know," the middle section "Want to Know," and the bottom section "Learned."

2. During the session, split participants into small groups. Give each group a KWL chart and a marker, and have group members fill in the "Know" and "Want to Know" sections.

3. Invite each small group to share its ideas with the large group.

4. At the end of the session, instruct the small groups to finish their charts by filling in the "Learned" section.

SHARING AND LEARNING ENGAGEMENT STRATEGY: CIRCLE IN A CIRCLE OR LINE BY LINE

Use this strategy to introduce a new topic. Alternatively, you could use it as a review strategy at the end of a training session.

Materials

1 sticky note or index card per participant

pens or pencils

1. Give each participant a sticky note or index card (and a pen or pencil, if needed).

2. Have everyone write a definition for a term that you will discuss (or have discussed) during the training session, such as *positive interactions*.

3. Ask participants to form two circles, an inner and outer circle, with the participants paired up and facing each other. Each circle should have the same number of people, so you may have to join one of the circles if you have an uneven number of learners. **Adaptation:** Instruct participants to form two lines facing each other.

4. Explain that the people across from each other are now partners, and invite the partnerships to share with each other what they have written.

5. After a few minutes, direct everyone in the outside circle to move two spaces to the right. Encourage participants to share what they wrote with their new partners.

6. Repeat three times.

SHARING AND LEARNING ENGAGEMENT STRATEGY: THE SYNONYM GAME

Having participants think of synonyms can broaden their perspectives.

1. Before the training session, create a PowerPoint slide with about eight words that teachers might commonly use in an early childhood classroom, such as *tired*, *hungry*, and *happy*.

2. Ask participants to think of synonyms for each word. Give participants time to write down their ideas, and then invite a few people to share ideas for each word.

3. Lead a whole-group discussion on how teachers can enhance young children's vocabulary by using a variety of words that have similar meanings. Explain that children benefit when they hear, for example, that they are *cheerful*, *merry*, *joyous*, and *exuberant* instead of just *happy*.

SHARING AND LEARNING ENGAGEMENT STRATEGY: SMALL-GROUP SHARE

This strategy spreads ideas from one group to another for discussion.

Materials

1 index card per participant

pens or pencils

1. After a presentation on a specific topic, give each participant an index card (and a pen or pencil, if needed).

2. Ask participants to respond on their cards to specific prompts, such as, "What types of activities are meaningful for children?" or "What roles should teachers take during center time?"

3. Split the participants into small groups.

4. Have each group gather up its cards and pass them to another group.

5. Direct the groups to read and discuss the answers on their new cards.

6. Bring the large group back together, and then ask several participants to share their insights from their small-group discussions

SHARING AND LEARNING ENGAGEMENT STRATEGY: STICKY-NOTE POLL

This strategy provides an interesting way to poll a group and determine people's preferences. For example, if you are training preschool teachers, you could list three different learning centers and ask each participant to choose a favorite.

Materials

sticky notes

pens or pencils

3 signs, each listing a different option

3 sheets of flip-chart paper

markers

1. Prior to the training session, post the signs on a wall.

2. During the training session, give each person a sticky note (and a pen or pencil, if needed). Instruct her to write her name on it, choose one (and only one) of the options, and post her sticky note under that sign.

3. Request that participants form small groups according to their votes.

4. Give each group a sheet of flip-chart paper and a marker. Instruct group members to discuss why they chose what they did and to record their top five reasons on their charts.

5. Invite each group to share its reasons with the other groups

Sticky-note polls also work well with children. Teachers can have children vote on a favorite activity or animal. During this type of activity, children can practice writing their names. Teachers can also extend the activity by helping children count how many people voted for each choice and compare which categories had the most and fewest votes.

SHARING AND LEARNING ENGAGEMENT STRATEGY: THE CONTINUUM

Use this strategy to quickly gauge the opinion of the group on different issues.

1. Give two extremes, such as process art and product art, and ask participants to think about where they would place themselves on the continuum between those extremes.

2. The participants create a human continuum by lining up according to where they stand on the issue.

3. Then discuss the topic as a large group or in small groups.

VIDEOS

The right video touches a learner's heart and mind. Videos provide visual examples, and exemplary ones can serve as discussion prompts. Some videos offer a variety of voices on a subject, such as when multiple experts share their thoughts on early childhood environments.

Videos can also prompt reflection and help learners better understand a topic. However, videos can also have drawbacks, so use the following guidelines to choose and use videos wisely.

CRITERIA FOR SELECTING VIDEOS

If you decide to use videos in a training session, this strategy needs to be intentional and purposeful. Consider these questions when selecting videos:

- Will the video appeal to a wide variety of adult learners?

- Does the video clearly demonstrate the desired teaching strategy or concept for the learners?

- Does the video meet my learning objectives?

- Is the video an appropriate length? (Usually two minutes or shorter is best.)

- Is the video high quality (has adequate light and sound, is in focus, and so on)?

- How current is the video? Does it reflect current research and styles? (Outdated clothing styles or antiquated technology can distract learners and diminish the value of a video.)

- Does the video demonstrate best practices?

- Can participants relate to the video? Is the cast diverse?

- Is a transcript available? Does the video have accessibility features, such as closed captioning? (Check captions ahead of time—some captions do not accurately reflect what is happening in the video or are only available in certain languages.)

- Is the video free, or must you pay to use it?

SHOWING AND SUPPORTING CONCEPTS

Videos provide a multisensory way to demonstrate, clarify, and reinforce concepts. Early childhood professionals learn by watching other teachers and pondering their actions. For example, Jia may struggle to understand how to use parallel talk in her classroom. However, after watching a video of another toddler teacher using this practice, Jia knows what the practice looks and sounds like, so she can better visualize how she can use it. As Jia discusses the video with her peers, they collectively identify the positive elements of the video example. Then, through role play, Jia practices using parallel talk with a partner.

One powerful way to use videos is to ask participants to look for certain elements while watching. This activity can vividly illustrate the concept or practice you are teaching. For example, one trainer showed a series of clips of the same child at different ages from infant to toddler to two years old. She asked the participants to focus on the child's language development as they watched. The learners noticed that child's language abilities expanded significantly at certain ages. This video sequence provided a memorable lesson because the videos clearly demonstrated the child's development over time.

Similarly, you might show a clip of several children engaged in play and ask one group of participants to watch the clip through a physical-development lens, another group to watch through a social-emotional-development lens, and a third group to watch through a cognitive-development lens. Then small groups of participants could discuss what they noticed through each lens. Alternatively, you could show the same clip multiple times so participants could practice looking for different elements or deepen their understanding.

If training participants are attending multiple sessions, you could give them a video homework assignment. Start by selecting a video library that has a search feature. Give each participant a topic, such as teacher-child interactions, and ask everyone to find a short clip that demonstrates that topic. At the next training session, select several individuals to share their clips, why they chose those clips, and what each clip demonstrates about the topic.

PROMPTING REFLECTION

Videos can lead teachers to think about their own practices as they watch other teachers work. For example, one trainer had training participants watch a video of a teacher interacting with four children and a basket of interesting objects. The trainer then asked everyone to reflect on both the teacher's and the children's actions.

Following the reflection time, the trainer asked several people to comment on their reflections. One person commented on the types of unique materials that the children were drawn to within the basket. Another person stated that the teacher in the video was calm and encouraging but not overpowering during her interactions with the children. The trainer then challenged the group to create a list of materials that they could place in a basket to interest the children in their classrooms. In this way, the video provided a springboard for reflection and discussion.

To prompt even deeper reflection, consider asking adult learners to bring in video clips from their own classrooms (remind them to obtain the appropriate parental permission slips first).

By viewing themselves in action, teachers gain great insights about their practices. While teaching, a teacher is in the middle of an experience, but when she watches a video of herself teaching, her brain can get a broader view of the situation and quickly think of ways to enhance children's experiences.

For instance, a video was taken of one teacher during story time. In the video, the assistant teachers constantly moved eager children away from the limited number of props that the teacher was using for the story. As the teacher watched the video, she said, "We need to divide the children into smaller groups, and I need more props for them!" This video quickly showed the teacher how she could improve her practice and increase the children's engagement during story time.

Case Study: Using a Video Effectively

During one training session I attended, the trainer showed a video of a preschool boy filling a cardboard oatmeal container at a water table. He began to carry the container away, but the bottom ripped open, sending water pouring out. There was an audible gasp from the audience. What a mess!

The trainer stopped the video and had us think about how we would react if this situation occurred in our classrooms. Small groups of participants discussed ideas. Then the trainer resumed the video. The teacher in the video calmly came over and talked to the child about what had happened. She asked the child if he was surprised and what he had learned from the experience.

This experience demonstrates how a well-chosen and well-used video can enhance a training session. Because the trainer paused and gave the group time to think about what they would do, the video gave participants the opportunity to reflect on their own practices. Then the video went on to positively demonstrate a best practice that participants could implement.

TIPS FOR MAKING THE MOST OF VIDEOS

- When you consider using a video in a training presentation, make sure to watch the entire video before you decide to use it.

- Avoid showing videos that illustrate inappropriate practices. Even if you have a discussion about the example and why it is inappropriate, participants may remember the video and not the discussion.

- If you decide to use a longer video, break it into smaller chunks. Watch a short segment, pause, and discuss what is happening. Then ask participants to predict how they think the teacher in the video will act before you go on.

- Be respectful to the people in the video by keeping the discussion positive. Teachers who are willing to be videotaped are taking a risk: they are allowing others to scrutinize their actions. Most teachers are doing the best they can in their current situations. Therefore, we need to be respectful of them, just as we would want them to be respectful of us if we had been videotaped. To this end, ask participants to view the video through a strengths-based lens. Pose questions such as these:
    - What was the teacher doing well?
    - What can we learn from the video?
    - How can we apply this example into our own teaching of young children?

For a list of websites with useful early childhood videos, see appendix O.

VIDEOS FOR A FLIPPED CLASSROOM

If you conduct multiple training sessions with the same group, you can use videos as part of a flipped classroom. This strategy provides instructional content to students through a virtual platform outside of the classroom. For example, you might assign adult learners to watch several videos before they come to the next training session. Then during the next session, small groups of participants can discuss what they viewed.

BRAIN BREAKS

If you notice that your participants are looking glassy eyed, it is time for a brain break. Brain breaks are quick ways to refresh participants' minds. But you do not have to wait for people to doze off—you can strategically plan brain breaks throughout your training sessions. Brain breaks typically include some type of physical activity or movement. Here are some ideas:

• Have everyone stand up and do some stretches.

• Ask each participant to stand up and touch her right ear with her left hand and her nose with her right hand. Then have her switch so that the right hand touches the left ear and the left hand touches the nose. Tell everyone to switch several more times.

• Direct everyone to stand up, touch her nose with her right index finger, and lift her left foot off the ground. Then instruct everyone to switch so that she touches her nose with her left index finger and lifts her right foot off the ground. Ask everyone if one position felt more balanced. Then have each participant put both feet on the ground, touch her head with both hands, and close her eyes. Ask, "How does it feel?"

• Tell each person to pretend she has a giant pencil with a suction cup on one end. Ask everyone to stick the suction cup on her forehead and "write" a word related to your training topic (such as *science*) with her giant pencil. Then instruct everyone to remove the suction cup from her forehead, move the suction cup to one hip, and "write" another word related to the training topic (such as *explore*). Then direct everyone to remove the suction cup from her hip, move the suction cup to one elbow, and "write" the answer to a question about the training topic (such as, "What is a favorite material in your science center?").

• Play non-elimination Simon Says. Explain that participants should only follow the directions that begin with "Simon says." Call out different directions, some prefaced with "Simon says" and others not—for example, "Turn around," or "Simon says touch the top of your head." If someone does an action that did not begin with "Simon says," ask that person to face backwards until she correctly follows a "Simon says" direction; then she can turn forward again. This rule adds an extra element of fun, and no one is eliminated from participating in the game.

• This brain break requires focus and concentration and is also a lot of fun! Have everyone find a partner. Ask partners to face each other and alternate counting back and forth to three. For example, Person A says, "One"; Person B says, "Two"; Person A says, "Three"; Person B says, "One" and so on. Often Person B will want to say, "Four" instead of "One." Once the group has mastered this counting pattern, ask everyone to continue counting back and forth with increasing numbers of substitutions:

    • Clap instead of saying, "Two" (so the pattern becomes "One," clap, "Three," "One," clap, "Three," and so on)

    • Snap instead of saying, "One" (snap, clap, "Three," snap, clap, "Three," and so on)

    • Stomp instead of saying, "Three" (snap, clap, stomp, snap, clap, stomp, and so on)

- Teach participants an action for each vowel (*A, E, I, O,* and *U*). Then either post or call out sets of vowels (such as *I, A, U*), and have participants do the actions in the corresponding order. Continue for several rounds. Here are some example actions for each vowel:
    - A: wave arms and say, "Ehhhh!"
    - E: shake hands as if scared and say, "Eeee!"
    - I: point to eyes and say, "Eyyyyye!"
    - O: draw a giant circle with arms and say, "Oooooh!"
    - U: point to someone else and say, "Yooooou!"
- Put on a video of a children's song or fingerplay that includes actions, and have everyone move to the music and sing or recite along.

Be creative! Brain breaks are a great way to rejuvenate the mind and the body during training sessions.

REFLECTION STRATEGIES

Reflection involves taking time to think, ponder, and contemplate. It often leads adult learners to new insights. Try these strategies to promote reflection during your training sessions.

REFLECTION ENGAGEMENT STRATEGY: PICTURE THAT!

This strategy generates a lot of discussion. Just looking at photos of children always brings smiles to participants' faces.

Materials

photos of children showing a variety of facial expressions, such as happy, sad, angry, and surprised (you can find great photos at pixabay.com)

Example for Training Classroom Teachers

1. Place participants in pairs or small groups, and distribute the photos.

2. Have participants look at the photos and identify the emotions each child is expressing.

3. Ask the pairs or small groups to discuss how children's facial cues communicate their emotions. Then bring the whole group together and discuss the main points of the small-group discussions.

Example for Training Coaches

1. Place participants in pairs or small groups, and distribute the photos.

2. Have participants look at the photos and identify the emotions each child is expressing.

3. Suggest that participants reflect on how they feel when they are coaching and how the people they coach might feel during coaching.

4. Ask each person to select two photos: one that represents how she feels as a coach and one that represents how someone she coaches might feel. Some coaches like to pick a "before"

picture (someone who is just starting coaching) and an "after" picture (someone who has been coached for a while).

5. Have participants share with their partners or groups which photos they picked and why.

6. Bring the whole group together, and ask several people to share their photos with the larger group.

New coaches often select a photo of a child who looks overwhelmed for either themselves or the people they are coaching.

REFLECTION ENGAGEMENT STRATEGY: FOUR CORNERS

Materials

4 sheets of flip-chart paper

markers

4 pictures related to your prompt (see examples at the end of the instructions)

1. Prior to the activity, post a sheet of flip-chart paper and a picture in each corner of the room. Leave the markers near the charts.

2. Present a prompt to the group, and ask each participant to go to the chart with the picture that represents her answer.

3. Have the resulting groups write their reasoning on the charts and then share it with the large group.

Example for Training Coaches

Prompt: Coaching is most like:

• a picnic in the park.

• a trip to the zoo.

• a three-act play.

• a tennis match.

Here are some possible responses:

• Coaching is like a tennis match because there is a lot of back and forth between the coach and the teacher.

Analogies promote creative thought processes.

• Coaching is like a three-act play because there can be a lot of drama in a coaching relationship. During the first act, the characters are introduced. During the second act, conflict arises and the characters change. In the final act, the conflict is resolved and the characters celebrate the positive outcome as the curtain closes.

Example on the Topic of Change

This prompt leads to insightful responses, showing who wants to hide in a hole like a mouse, go slowly and steadily like a turtle, fight back like a lion, or speed ahead like a racehorse when it comes to change.

Prompt: When I think about change, I am most like . . .

- a mouse.

- a turtle.

- a lion.

- a racehorse.

REFLECTION ENGAGEMENT STRATEGY: GRAFFITI FENCE
Materials

long piece of butcher paper

markers

1. Prior to the training session, draw a picket fence with wide posts on the butcher paper. Post the paper on the wall and leave the markers nearby. **Adaptation:** Create a graffiti wall by using a blank piece of butcher paper.

2. Ask participants a question, such as, "If you could change one thing in your classroom environment, what would you do?" or "What is an important issue in early childhood education?"

3. Have participants reflect on the question and illustrate their responses on the graffiti fence with pictures and words.

4. Discuss some of the ideas on the fence with the large group.

5. Split the participants into small groups, and instruct them to discuss how they could implement the listed ideas or how they could persuade decision makers to act on the ideas.

REFLECTION ENGAGEMENT STRATEGY: PROVOCATION

A *provocation* catalyzes the imagination to think about new ideas. It is an open-ended activity with interesting materials, often from nature, that inspire children and adults to explore, create, and invent.

Materials

open-ended items such as kinetic sand, clay, shells, beads, framed artwork, paints, chalk, paper, blank picture frames, leaves, flowers, thread spools, rocks, colored stones, or wood pieces

1. Before the training session, set out the materials on small tables around the room.

2. At the appropriate time in the session, invite participants to explore the items. If participants have difficulties getting started, suggest some ways to engage with the materials.

3. Bring the group back together, and ask everyone to reflect on the experience.

4. Lead a whole-group discussion about the experience, how it relates to teaching young children, and how novel and open-ended materials create interest and promote creativity.

REFLECTION ENGAGEMENT STRATEGY: MY SOCIAL-EMOTIONAL PORTRAIT

This activity works well during a training session on the social-emotional development of young children. As teachers reflect on their own social-emotional portraits, they begin to gain a greater understanding of themselves and the children they teach.

Materials

1 copy of "My Social-Emotional Portrait" handout per participant (see appendix P)

pens or pencils

1. Distribute the handouts (and pens or pencils, if needed).

2. Explain that each participant will create her own social-emotional portrait by filling in the sections on the handout:

   • In "Enjoyable Social Activity," she lists a social activity that she enjoys.

   • In "BFF (Best Friend Forever)," she writes the name of her BFF.

   • In "Describe Your Happy Place," she lists details about her "happy place" or some other place where she likes to spend time.

   • In "Emotions," she writes several emotions that she has felt while teaching.

   • In "Fear," she describes something that she fears (such as snakes or heights).

3. Ask each participant to reflect on her social-emotional portrait and how it influences her interactions with young children.

4. Divide participants into small groups, and have group members share their social-emotional portraits with each other.

5. Invite a few participants to share their portraits with the large group.

6. Lead a whole-group discussion about the concepts of friendship, emotions, and fears as they relate to children and early childhood professionals.

REFLECTION ENGAGEMENT STRATEGY: RANK IT!

This strategy requires participants to think about research and statistics related to the early childhood profession.

Materials

1 set of word strips per group

1. Prior to the training session, create the word-strip sets. Each strip should list a different research-based statement related to early childhood (such as a statistic about infant or toddler care). **Adaptation**: List individual steps in a process, such as changing a diaper, on each word strip.

2. Split the participants into small groups, and give each group a set of word strips.

3. Instruct participants to reflect on the statements and think about how pertinent each statement is to early childhood.

4. Have the small groups discuss the statements and then rank them from most to least pertinent. **Adaptation:** If you put individual steps on each word strip, tell participants to put the strips in the correct order.

REFLECTION ENGAGEMENT STRATEGY: STICKY-NOTE COMPLETION PROMPTS

Materials

1 sheet of flip-chart paper

pens or pencils

sticky notes

1. Before the training session, write a prompt (such as, "Positive guidance is . . .") at the top of a sheet of flip-chart paper, and post the chart on the wall.

2. During the session, give each participant a sticky note (and a pen or pencil, if needed) and ask her to complete the prompt.

3. Depending on the size of the group and how much time you want to spend on the activity, you can proceed in two different ways:

   - Invite each person to come to the front of the room, read her sticky note aloud, and place it on the chart.

   - Have participants pair up or form small groups, share with each other what they wrote, and then place their sticky notes on the chart. When everyone finishes, ask a few participants to share what they wrote with the large group or highlight a few of the main ideas on the chart.

REFLECTION ENGAGEMENT STRATEGY: SORTING CONCEPTS

Sometimes participants struggle to identify whether an example does or does not apply to the concept you are teaching. This activity can provide clarification.

Materials

1 set of word strips per group

1 paper titled "Yes" per group

1 paper titled "No" per group

1. Prior to the training session, create word strips with statements that are and are not examples of the concept you are teaching. For example, you could have descriptions of practices that are and are not effective transitions, or you could have some word strips that list health and safety tips and other word strips that list actual state standards for these areas. Create papers titled "Yes" and "No" so participants can sort the word strips.

2. During the training session, split participants into groups, and give each group a set of word strips and papers.

3. Direct participants to read each word strip and reflect on whether the practice is or is not an example of the concept they have just learned.

4. Have participants discuss each statement and sort the word strips by placing each one on the appropriate paper.

5. Discuss with the participants why they sorted each word strip as they did.

REFLECTION ENGAGEMENT STRATEGY: STICKY-NOTE COMMENTS

Use this activity to increase engagement when groups of learners present information. This strategy leads to purposeful listening.

Materials

1 sheet of flip-chart paper per group

markers

sticky notes

pens or pencils

1. Split participants into small groups, and give each group a sheet of flip-chart paper and a marker.

2. Instruct the small groups to prepare presentations, using their charts to write their main ideas or draw visuals, or both.

3. Before the presentations begin, give each participant enough sticky notes so that she has one sticky note for each group that will be presenting (and a pen or pencil, if needed).

4. Before a group presents, ask each participant to listen to the presentation, reflect on the information that she hears, and then write a comment or a piece of feedback for the presenters on one of her sticky notes.

5. At the end of a presentation, have the listeners place their sticky notes around the edges of that group's chart.

6. After everyone has presented, instruct group members to read the comments on the sticky notes and to discuss the feedback with each other.

REFLECTION ENGAGEMENT STRATEGY: WHICH ONE DOESN'T BELONG?

This activity promotes reflection by highlighting different perspectives and thought processes. Try it during a training session on a topic such as math, cognitive development, or open-mindedness.

Materials

1 copy of chosen puzzle per group (optional)

1. Prior to the training session, visit the website http://wodb.ca/ and choose a puzzle to print out or add to your PowerPoint. Notice that answers are not provided for the puzzles, as there are a variety of ways of selecting which item does not belong.

2. During the training session, distribute the hard copies of the puzzle or show the applicable slide from your PowerPoint.

3. Ask participants to reflect individually on which item does not belong and why. Then have participants form small groups and discuss their ideas.

4. Invite a few small groups to share their ideas with the large group. Remind participants that there are no right or wrong answers.

REFLECTION ENGAGEMENT STRATEGY: TRANSITIONS GAME

Board games can effectively teach concepts and simulate early childhood experiences. I created this game to use in training sessions about transitions in preschool classrooms. It worked particularly well to help participants feel the frustration that children may experience in classrooms with too many transitions and extended wait times.

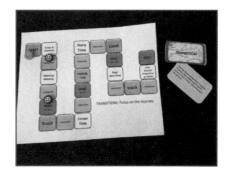

Materials

1 game board per group

1 set of Transition Cards per group

1 playing piece per participant (such as small erasers)

1 die per group

1 set of game instructions per group

Game Instructions

1. All playing pieces begin on the Start space.

2. Players roll the die to determine who goes first (highest result wins). Play then proceeds in a clockwise direction.

3. On her turn, a player rolls the die. On a 1 or a 2, she advances her playing piece the applicable number of spaces. On a 3, 4, 5, or 6, she must wait and pass the die to the next player.

4. If a player lands on a Wait space, she loses a turn.

5. When a player lands on a Transition space, she must draw a Transition Card. If the action on the card provides an effective transition, the player moves forward the number of spaces listed on the card. If the action on the card keeps children waiting, the player moves backward the number of spaces listed on the card.

6. The first player to reach the Finish space wins. (The player does not need to land on Finish by exact count, and players rarely finish the game within the given time frame.)

How to Use the Game

1. Split participants into groups of four, and distribute the game materials.

2. Instruct participants to begin playing. In my experience, after about ten minutes, participants begin complaining that they can't finish the game because there are too many Wait spaces and ineffective transitions!

3. After about fifteen minutes of play, stop the game.

4. Lead a whole-group discussion about transitions and wait times in early childhood classrooms. Discuss how it felt to wait. Did anyone feel frustrated and want to stop playing? How does this game relate to transitions in early childhood classrooms?

REVIEW STRATEGIES

Use these strategies at various times throughout a training session to review the information that you have presented.

REVIEW STRATEGY: KNOW, TRY, CIRCLING IN MY HEAD

Materials

1 sheet of lined paper per participant

pens or pencils

1 sheet of flip-chart paper per group

markers

1. After discussing a topic, distribute the paper (and pen or pencil, if needed) and have each participant write down these items:

   - One idea that represents something she now *knows* about the topic

   - One idea that she would like to *try*

   - One idea that is still *circling in her head*

2. Ask participants to form small groups. Give each group a sheet of flip-chart paper and a marker, and instruct them to write their ideas on their charts.

3. Invite each small group to share with the main group.

REVIEW STRATEGY: CREATE A HEADLINE

This exercise forces participants to drill down to the essence of what they have learned. When introducing this activity, you may want to give a few examples to help participants get started.

Materials

1 sheet of lined paper per group

pens or pencils

1. Split participants into small groups. Give each group a sheet of paper (and a pen or pencil, if needed).

2. Assign each group to write a headline (a short statement that highlights the main idea) to summarize what they have learned.

3. Invite each small group to share its headline with the large group.

REVIEW STRATEGY: CREATE AN INFOGRAPHIC

An infographic communicates information using primarily graphics, symbols, and key words. It helps if you provide some examples when introducing this activity.

Materials

1 sheet of flip-chart paper per group

markers

1. Split participants into small groups. Give each group a sheet of flip-chart paper and some markers.

2. Instruct group members to summarize their thoughts and ideas about a specific topic by adding graphics, symbols, and key words to a piece of flip-chart paper.

3. Invite each small group to share its infographic with the large group.

REVIEW STRATEGY: INTERLOCKING BLOCKS

Using interlocking blocks provides a fun way to review. This strategy works best if the concepts from your training session fit into categories. For example, if you are training on developmental milestones for toddlers, your word strips could include milestones related to children's cognitive, social-emotional, physical, and language development.

Materials

large interlocking blocks

word strips

tape

1. Prior to the training session, create word strips with concepts related to the training topic, and tape them to the interlocking blocks. Place main concepts on larger blocks and subsidiary concepts on smaller blocks. For larger groups, create multiple sets of blocks with the same words and headings.

2. During the training session, after presenting the applicable content, ask the participants to review what they have learned by building towers. If the group is large, split the participants into smaller groups.

3. Distribute the blocks.

4. Direct participants to create towers by using each of the main concepts as a base and adding subsidiary concepts on top of them.

Adaptation: Use a single set of blocks. Before the training session, scatter the blocks on participants' tables throughout the room. During the session, ask a participant to bring each block to the front of the room when the topic on that block is discussed. As the session progresses, the participants create a tower of knowledge.

REVIEW STRATEGY: EXIT TICKET

An exit ticket provides helpful insights about what adult learners consider the most important takeaway from a training session.

Materials

1 exit ticket per participant (see appendix **Q**)

pens or pencils

1. At the end of the training session, distribute the exit tickets (and pens or pencils, if needed).

2. Ask participants to fill out the tickets and give them (and any borrowed pens or pencils) to you as they leave the room.

3. If you hold a later training session with the same group, at the beginning of the next session, remind each person of what she wrote on her exit ticket. Invite learners to discuss how they have applied what they wrote on their exit tickets into their classroom practices since the previous session.

REVIEW STRATEGY: CIRCLE SUMMARY COMMITMENT

At the end of a training session, you can use this activity to make a final connection with participants.

1. Ask everyone to form a circle.

2. Explain that one of the best ways to change practices is to verbally commit to someone else that one will make certain changes.

3. Instruct each participant to turn to the person next to her and share something she learned during the training session and how she will take that new knowledge back and implement it in her classroom or program. **Extension:** If the session is part of an ongoing series, build time into the next session for participants to share what they actually did.

CHAPTER 13:

Addressing Challenging Behavior in Adult Learners

Thana is leading a training session. One participant, Kevin, talks frequently and cuts off other participants when they speak, so most participants stop commenting. Thana tries directing questions to a specific person, but Kevin begins interrupting the chosen speakers and interjecting his ideas. Finally, Thana invites everyone to form small groups and discuss a question. Meanwhile, she asks Kevin to speak with her in the hall.

First, Thana thanks Kevin for sharing his thoughts. Then she explains that his eagerness is preventing other participants from speaking, and she asks him how they can solve this issue. Seeming surprised, Kevin apologizes. Thana accepts the apology and reminds him of the group guideline of having all voices heard. She promises to provide time in the session for participants to share personal experiences and asks Kevin to ensure that others are finished before he speaks. He agrees, and they return to class.

CHALLENGE ACCEPTED

Trainers also frequently encounter challenging behaviors from adult learners. Some learners are disruptive, talkative, or critical. Participants may arrive late or refuse to participate. Some people may even text or shop online during training sessions!

When these types of behavior occur, what do you do? You can ignore some of these behaviors, but you need to address others. In this chapter, we examine two categories of strategies for dealing with challenging behavior: prevention strategies and management strategies.

PREVENTION STRATEGIES

The best strategy for dealing with challenging behavior is prevention. Try these ideas to keep difficulties from occurring in the first place:

- Prepare in advance and be ready to go at your appointed start time.
- Set clear behavior expectations at the beginning of each training session, and reinforce them throughout the session.

- Also at the beginning of each training session, provide specific guidelines for respectful engagement, such as sharing the floor and being open to different viewpoints. Have participants verbally agree to follow the guidelines.

- Show confidence and enthusiasm to promote a positive atmosphere. Your behavior sets the tone for the class and is key to establishing an emotionally safe climate.

- Use a variety of engagement strategies.

- To reduce the number of side conversations, provide opportunities for group discussions.

- Establish classroom norms, such as these:

    - Start and end training sessions on time.

    - Turn off or silence cell phones.

    - Save texting for breaks.

    - Respect others' contributions.

    - Stay on topic.

    - Resolve differences in a calm and professional manner.

MANAGEMENT STRATEGIES

Sometimes, despite your best efforts at prevention, challenging behaviors still occur. Let's examine some common issues and how to address them.

TALKING

Talking can disrupt training sessions in two main ways. First, a single participant might give lengthy answers to questions or dominate the discussion. Second, small groups of participants might engage in side conversations. Each situation requires different strategies.

Talkers Who Dominate Discussions

Try these strategies to keep one person from doing all the talking:

- Reiterate group guidelines related to sharing the floor.

- When you ask the group a question, say, "I'd like to hear from someone who hasn't answered a question."

- Call on people in various areas of the room.

- Have learners discuss their thoughts in pairs. Then call on specific individuals to share their ideas.

- Teach learners to use protocols that give everyone an opportunity to speak. Have participants practice these protocols by discussing a topic in small groups. Assign a facilitator for each group to make sure everyone follows the protocols.

- Tactfully redirect the dominating talker by stopping him, thanking him for his thoughts, and changing the topic. For example, you might say, "Sam, I'm going to stop you. Thank you for sharing that important point—we do need to remember to pay attention to what children are saying and doing. We're now going to talk about . . ."

- Set a word limit for responses. For instance, ask participants to summarize their ideas in twenty words or fewer.

- Split the main group into small groups and tell everyone that he can give his two cents—an idiom for "his opinion"—on the discussion topic. Give each person two coins and explain that each time a person speaks, he needs to place a coin in the center of the table. All group members need to give their two cents on the topic before anyone speaks a third time.

- Begin a large-group discussion by stating, "I'd like to hear from as many people as possible, so make your responses clear and concise."

- Before a participant gives a response, say, "Let's all listen to what [the person's name] is going to say."

Side Conversations

Side conversations may indicate that participants need more opportunities to talk to each other. These strategies may prove helpful:

- Build partner and small-group discussions and regular breaks into the schedule.

- Ask the side talkers if they would like to share with the rest of the group.

- Stop speaking and look right at the side talkers. Smile at them until they stop talking.

- Move closer to the side talkers and stand by them until they notice and stop talking.

- Politely ask side talkers to wait until a break to talk to each other.

- Use a noisemaker to get the group's attention. Then say something like this: "Natsuo is going to speak. Let's all be respectful and listen to what he has to say."

- Ask the side talkers to rejoin the group discussion: "We need to have everyone contributing to this conversation."

- Talk to the entire group about how side conversations are distracting. Ask the group to brainstorm solutions for addressing the issue

GOING OFF TOPIC

Sometimes participants share stories and information that do not relate to the topic of the training session. They may also ask questions that are highly specific to their own situations and not applicable to the larger group. These strategies may help you get back on track:

- Before the session begins, set up a "parking lot" by posting a sheet of flip-chart paper where anyone can write down ideas and questions that do not directly relate to the current topic. You can then address those thoughts later, either with the whole group or individually.

- Tell the individual with the off-topic idea that you will address his thought later in the session or after class.

- Ask the participant to share how his story or information is related to the training topic. Sometimes what we think is off topic may not be.

- Redirect the conversation by asking others if they have anything to add related to the topic.

NEGATIVITY

Negativity can affect the atmosphere of a training session. Some learners question everything you say or repeatedly protest, "That'll never work in my classroom!" Others complain about you or your methods and insist that they could train better. Still others may not verbalize their feelings, but you can tell from their folded arms, frowns, and lack of participation that they would rather not be at your training session. Here are some ideas for dealing with this type of behavior:

- When a participant makes a negative comment, remain calm and professional, and do not take the comment personally. Validate the person's ideas by saying, "I appreciate you sharing your point of view. What do others think?"

- A negative comment can actually reveal a problem that the participant needs help solving. In this type of situation, consider having the group brainstorm solutions to the issue. The participant may more willingly receive ideas from his peers than from you.

- Try restating a negative comment using positive phrasing. For example, if a participant says, "That'll never work," you could say, "It sounds like you think this will be a challenge."

- Ask the participant to share what is working in his classroom.

- During a break, privately check in with the person to see if he is okay. He may not be feeling well or may be struggling with personal issues.

- Talk to the person privately and share your concerns about how his behavior affects the other learners.

ARGUING AND CRITICISM

Sometimes challenging behavior goes beyond negativity. Some participants like to argue with you and criticize the information you present. Try these strategies to defuse such situations:

- Validate the critic's concerns and move on.

- Remain calm and professional. Stay in control of your own behavior.

- Sometimes the best response is to ask the critic, "What do *you* think you could do?" You may need to be persistent and keep pressing for a response related to something that the critic thinks *could* work in his situation.

- Ask other participants for their ideas.

- Engage the group in a healthy discussion about how different points of view can coexist.

- Challenge adult learners to advocate for the opposites of their personal opinions to gain other perspectives on the issue.

- Have participants list the pros and cons of different solutions.

- Use concrete examples, statistics, research articles, and data to support the information you present.

- If the behavior becomes too disruptive, give the group a break. Then privately talk to the critic and respectfully ask him to change his behavior or leave the training session.

ATTENDANCE ISSUES

Adult learners sometimes arrive late or leave early. Some participants take extended breaks or leave the training space multiple times during a training session. All these behaviors can disrupt other participants' learning. Try these strategies to minimize these disruptions:

- Find out whether your district or state has an established attendance policy for training sessions. If a policy exists, enforce it.

- Post your attendance policy on the door of your training space.

- If you will be holding a series of training sessions, such as the coursework for the Child Development Associate credential, have participants sign the attendance policy prior to the beginning of the course. The policy should clearly outline what a participant must do if he misses a session. Depending on your program and the training guidelines in your state, you can determine whether and how missed sessions can be made up. For example, a participant who misses an in-person session could make it up by taking an online class on the same topic.

- Talk to the person outside of class and state your concerns. Find out why he has had irregular attendance. Remind him that his behavior affects other class participants, and work together for an acceptable solution.

- Be careful to not reward latecomers by repeating what they missed. Inform latecomers that you will meet with them during a break or after class to briefly discuss what they missed.

- If someone tells you ahead of time that he needs to leave early, state your policy on whether he will receive credit for attending the session. Ask him to leave quietly and with as little disruption as possible when the time comes.

SHY, RESERVED, OR RELUCTANT PARTICIPANTS

Some adult learners do not feel comfortable sharing their thoughts and ideas or being in large groups. Although you should respect each person's preferences for interactions, try some of these strategies to encourage these learners to participate:

- Involve shy participants through partner and small-group discussions. Timid individuals may be more willing to share in these smaller settings.

- Provide time for participants to build trusting relationships with each other. Some individuals are more comfortable sharing with people they know.

- Privately ask the reserved person whether he would be comfortable sharing with the group if called upon.

- Give shy participants a question ahead of time so they have time to prepare their responses.

- In partnerships or groups that include reluctant participants, have the other group member or members share the reluctant individual's ideas.

- Avoid forcing participants to share if they do not feel comfortable doing so.

- Ask participants to write down ideas, organize their thoughts, and then share them with the group.

- Be patient. Sometimes participants will begin sharing once they feel emotionally safe within the group.

REFUSAL TO PARTICIPATE

Occasionally, adult learners simply refuse to participate in certain activities. You cannot force participation, but try these ideas to encourage these learners to get and stay involved:

- Allow the participant to just observe. Ask him if he would be willing to share what he observed later in the training session.

- Do not overreact. The person may be seeking attention or seeing how you will react to his refusal to participate. Sometimes it is best just to ignore the behavior and see if the participant opts to join in later.

- Respectfully encourage participation. For instance, you might say something like, "Devin, what do you think?"

- Set clear, simple limits. For instance, you could tell the participant that he needs to stay with his group and stay focused on the topic.

- Avoid engaging in a power struggle. For example, sometimes the more you encourage a person to participate, the more he resists and refuses to participate. In these cases, disengage with the person so that his behavior does not detract from the experiences of other participants.

- Be patient. Sometimes adult learners will participate when they finally feel comfortable with the group.

- Remember that adult learners may have health conditions, such as back problems, that prevent them from participating in certain activities.

DISRUPTIONS FROM ELECTRONIC DEVICES

During training sessions, adult learners might use their electronic devices for activities outside the scope of the session. You must determine for yourself what constitutes acceptable and unacceptable use of technology in your training sessions. Usually you can ignore the occasional side use of technology, such as a participant texting once during the session. But if a cell phone goes off every ten minutes or the light from a laptop distracts other participants, it is a good idea for you to talk to the disruptive devices' owners. Also, consider this: if cell phones, tablets, and laptops are more interesting than you are, you may want to make your presentation more engaging! In the meantime, try the following strategies to minimize technological distractions.

- Use a variety of engagement strategies throughout your training session.

- If needed, establish a cell-phone use policy. Clearly state what is acceptable and unacceptable. Be sensitive to real needs versus preferences—for instance, a participant may need to have his phone handy if he is expecting an important call or dealing with an emergency.

- Include regular breaks throughout the training session. Individuals feel less need to use their phones during a session if they know they have an upcoming break and can check for messages then.

- Have some fun! At the start of the session, playfully tell participants to hurry and check their phones for messages. Then ask everyone to silence their phones and put them away until a break.

- Have participants use their devices in a productive way during class, such as participating in online polls and response games.

- If phones become a real obstacle to participant engagement, you may need to set up a phone drop-off basket as learners enter the room!

CONFUSED PARTICIPANTS

Every trainer dreads finishing an explanation and meeting a sea of blank stares. Sometimes facial expressions or body language may be your only clues that adult learners are confused. Other times, participants tell you candidly that they have no idea what you are talking about. If your participants are not getting it, try these strategies to clarify:

- Encourage participants to ask questions and seek clarification as needed.

- Include videos, stories, and examples that demonstrate practices or concepts in action.

- Ask learners to summarize main points. Sometimes it helps participants to hear a peer restate what the trainer has already said.

- Assure participants that you are always ready to help—they just need to ask.

- Talk to participants privately and provide additional clarification during breaks and after class.

- Encourage, but do not force, participation, especially during small-group discussions.

- Ask the confused person to share in his own words what he does understand. His statements can help you determine what points need clarification.

- Use a strengths-based approach to learning. Focus on the positive qualities and contributions of each person instead of on the skills and abilities that participants may lack.

- Create an emotional climate that makes it safe for participants to seek help and ask questions.

- Offer to email the confused participant and provide additional resources on the topic.

- Differentiate your instruction to address a variety of levels of learners. For example, if a concept has a complex definition, give that definition first, and then illustrate the concept through verbal and visual examples that are easier to understand. You could also ask participants to work in small groups and discuss how the concept applies to their specific situations.

POWER SEEKERS AND KNOW-IT-ALLS

Some learners attempt to provoke you into battles of words and present themselves as experts on certain topics. These learners can cause immense frustration. Keep your cool and try these strategies:

- Avoid engaging in a power struggle or becoming defensive.

- Detach yourself, and do not take comments personally.

- Remain calm and professional.

- Direct attention to other members of the group.

- Move to a small-group activity.

- Speak to the person privately, if needed.

- Acknowledge and honor the participant's expertise: "That's a great idea. Thanks for sharing."

- Give the person a specific assignment to share information on a topic at a later time.

PRACTICE SCENARIOS

Try visualizing or role-playing these situations with a friend or supervisor. If you already have some idea of what you will do or say, you can better respond when challenging behaviors arise during actual training sessions. Here are some examples:

- Amber comes rushing into the room about twenty-five minutes late. She says, "I'm so sorry I'm late. I had car trouble, and the traffic was horrible, and I almost got in a wreck trying to get here on time."

- Ronaldo keeps glancing at his phone. He appears to be texting and looking at Facebook.

- You are leading a discussion on positive guidance strategies. Kiandra rolls her eyes as you speak, and when you finish, she shakes her head and says, "That would never work in my classroom! You have to tell children to stop. They only pay attention if you tell them no."

If you need additional support for dealing with challenging behaviors in adult learners, try meeting with other trainers to discuss ideas and share potential solutions.

- Cindy and Arjun start talking softly at first and then louder. Other participants look at them, but they are so involved in their conversation that they do not notice.

- Erhi stays extremely quiet and never shares any ideas. If you ask her a question, she mumbles a reply or says, "I don't know."

- Every time you ask a question, Regina calls out a long, detailed answer. You notice that other adult learners sigh, roll their eyes, or slouch in their chairs when she speaks.

- As you walk around the room during small-group discussions, you notice that Barry is dominating his group's conversation. His fellow group members seem to have no opportunity to share their ideas.

APPENDICES

Appendix A: Sample PLCs for Pre-K Teachers

Appendix B: Sample PLCs for Trainers and Coaches

Appendix C: Resources for a CoP on Leadership

Appendix D: "Your Leadership Journey" Handout

Appendix E: Recommended Leadership Books

Appendix F: Coach-Teacher Partnership Agreement

Appendix G: RSBC Conversation Planning Sheet

Appendix H: Plan of Action Geometric Form

Appendix I: RSBC Conversation Reflection Tool

Appendix J: RSBC Conversation Key Word Chart

Appendix K: Sample Training-Session Outline

Appendix L: Trainer Reflection Tool

Appendix M: "Clock Partners" Handout

Appendix N: "3, 2, 1" Handout

Appendix O: Video Resource List

Appendix P: "My Social-Emotional Portrait" Handout

Appendix Q: "Exit Ticket" Handout

APPENDIX A: SAMPLE PLCs FOR PRE-K TEACHERS

This appendix provides examples of topics and guiding questions that could be used in PLCs for pre-K teachers. You can adapt the suggested topics and questions to meet the specific needs of your PLC.

In the PLC from which these ideas come (see chapter 3), teachers would reflect on the questions prior to PLC sessions and then would discuss their responses in small groups during the sessions. The questions helped the teachers focus on ways to enhance learning-centers and experiences in their classrooms.

YEAR 1: ENHANCING LEARNING CENTERS AND EXPERIENCES

Topic	Guiding Questions
Setting the stage for dramatic play	What materials and props could you add to your dramatic-play area to enhance learning and represent diversity?
	Describe different themes you could add to your dramatic-play area throughout the year. How would these themes promote meaningful learning experiences for children?
Language and reasoning in pre-K classrooms	How could you set up opportunities throughout the day for children to develop their language and reasoning abilities?
	What types of books and other language and literacy materials could you add to your book area to enhance children's understanding of the world?
Math in pre-K classrooms	What types of daily activities could you implement in your classroom to promote children's understanding of math concepts?
	What types of teaching approaches could you use to challenge children's thinking and extend their math and numbers learning?
Nature and science in pre-K classrooms	How could you provide additional opportunities for children to explore the natural world?
	What types of natural items could you bring into your classroom to enhance children's scientific understanding?
How block play promotes development	What types of props and materials could you add to your block center to enhance learning and represent diversity?
	Describe different ways to promote children's higher-level thinking skills during block play.
Music and movement in pre-K classrooms	Describe the different types of music available to the children in your classroom. What could you add to increase the diversity of that music?
	What types of movement and dance activities could you include within your daily routines?
Sand and water play	What variations could you introduce to enhance sand and water play (such as adding water to sand play)?
	What materials could you add to sand and water play to promote children's exploration and experimentation?

YEAR 1: ENHANCING LEARNING CENTERS AND EXPERIENCES (continued)

Topic	Guiding Questions
The arts in pre-K classrooms	What materials, including three-dimensional art materials, could you add to your art area to promote creativity and individual expression?
	What art activities, including multiday projects, could you add to your curriculum that would connect to the concepts being taught and match the interests of the children in your classroom?
Promoting diversity in pre-K classrooms	What types of learning experiences could you include in your classroom to promote understanding and acceptance of diversity?
	Describe different types of play materials that you could use within a classroom to promote diversity.

YEAR 2: SOCIAL-EMOTIONAL DEVELOPMENT

During the second year of this PLC, the group members focused on practices related to implementing the Pyramid Model for Promoting Social Emotional Competence in Infants and Young Children. Participants received assessment data from the Teaching Pyramid Observation Tool (TPOT) for Preschool Classrooms to help guide their adjustments. Again, you can adapt these topics and questions to meet the specific needs of your PLC.

Topic	Guiding Questions
Schedules, routines, transitions, and activities	In what ways could you give extra support to children who struggle during routines, transitions, and activities?
	What strategies could you use to engage children during routines, transitions, and activities?
Engaging in supportive conversations	Give several examples of how you could offer a child positive, descriptive feedback.
	How could you enhance your conversations with children as you respond to their comments and questions?
Promoting children's engagement	How could you help children become actively engaged during center time? Be specific.
	What types of choices could you provide to children during large-group, small-group, and free-choice activities?
Teaching behavior expectations	How could you promote and link positive behavior to classroom behavior expectations?
	Give some examples of specific feedback that you could offer a child who meets behavior expectations.

Topic	Guiding Questions
Teaching social skills and emotional competencies	What activities could you implement with children to give them opportunities to cooperatively work together? Give several examples of how you could model and teach social skills and emotional competencies.
Teaching friendship skills	How could you model and help children practice using friendship skills? Give several examples of strategies and materials that you could use in your classroom to teach friendship skills (such as books about friendship skills or art projects that children complete in pairs).
Expressing emotions	How could you help children understand and talk about emotions? What strategies and materials (such as specific books or songs) could you use to teach children about emotions?
Teaching problem-solving skills	How could you teach children problem-solving skills? Give several examples of situations that you could use to help children practice problem-solving skills. These situations can be naturally occurring or created by the teacher.

APPENDIX B: SAMPLE PLCs FOR TRAINERS AND COACHES

These are examples of topics and guiding questions that facilitators can use to promote reflection and discussions during PLC sessions.

FOR TRAINERS: FACILITATING EFFECTIVE AND ENGAGING TRAINING SESSIONS

Topic	Guiding Questions
Adult learning principles	How could you base your training sessions on adult learning principles?
Addressing the needs of diverse learners	What strategies could you use to meet the needs of diverse adult learners? How can the languages, cultures, and abilities of adult learners influence your training sessions?
Becoming a confident and effective facilitator of learning	How could you become a confident and effective facilitator of learning?
Learning theories (such as experiential learning theory, constructivism, social learning theory, and the theory of multiple intelligences)	How could learning theories influence how you facilitate effective training sessions? What concepts from learning theories are applicable to training adult learners?
Engagement strategies	What types of engagement strategies could you use to introduce a topic, promote reflection, and help participants review information?
Making connections and building relationships	List three ways that you could make connections and build relationships with participants in your training sessions.
Multimodal instruction	In what ways could you utilize multimodal instruction to engage participants during a training session?
Presentation skills	What are your strengths and opportunities for growth in presentation skills?
Addressing challenging behavior in adult learners	What types of challenging behavior have you encountered in training sessions? What strategies could you use to address those behaviors?

FOR COACHES: REFLECTIVE STRENGTHS-BASED COACHING

Topic	Guiding Questions
Creating a coaching partnership	How could coaches develop coaching partnerships with teachers?
Engaging adult learners in reflection	What does *reflection* mean to you? How could you engage adult learners in reflection?
Building relationships	What strategies could you use to build relationships with individuals whom you are coaching?
Using guiding questions	What are some guiding questions that could promote reflection and expand learning in your coaching sessions?
Expanding learning	What strategies could you use to expand learning in your coaching sessions?
Changing practices	How could you guide the individuals you coach to change their teaching practices?
Ways to differentiate	How could you differentiate your coaching based on the unique needs of each person you coach?

APPENDIX C: RESOURCES FOR A CoP ON LEADERSHIP

This appendix provides examples of topics, books, reading assignments, and guiding questions that you could use to facilitate a CoP on leadership. During the sessions of the CoP from which these ideas come, participants had opportunities to discuss the guiding questions in small groups.

YEAR 1

Topic	Book	Reading Assignment	Guiding Questions
The power of positive, engaged leadership	*Leading Early Childhood Organizations* by Exchange Press	Subsection "Heart-Centered Leadership" in chapter 1 ("Being a Leader")	What does *positive, engaged leadership* mean to you? What is your long-term leadership vision? What are the characteristics of heart-centered leadership? How could you implement heart-centered leadership in your program?
Leading early childhood programs effectively	*Leading Early Childhood Organizations*	Subsection "Effective Leadership Behaviors" in chapter 1 ("Being a Leader")	What effective leadership behaviors do you currently have? What behaviors would you like to develop? What strengths and challenges do you have in communication and delegation?
Positive strengths-based supervision	*Leading Early Childhood Organizations*	Chapter 2: "Supervising Staff"	What do early childhood teachers need most from their directors? What positive, strengths-based supervision strategies do you currently use? What strategies would you like to start using? How could you help teachers "see" the real effects they have on children?
Strengthening relationships with your staff	*Leading Early Childhood Organizations*	Chapter 3: "Managing the Organization"	How do effective supervisors strengthen relationships with their staffs? How could you communicate authentically? How could you recognize your existing perceptions and biases and adopt a clean-slate perspective with your staff? How could you promote professionalism?
Selecting staff	*Developing People in Early Childhood Organizations* by Exchange Press	Chapter 1: "Selecting Staff"	What strategies could you use to hire qualified early childhood professionals? What questions and approaches are most effective during the interview process? How could you bring more diversity into your center?

Topic	Book	Reading Assignment	Guiding Questions
Intentional PL: training staff	*Developing People in Early Childhood Organizations*	Subsection "Helping Adults Succeed" from chapter 2 ("Training Staff")	How could you develop intentional, embedded PL opportunities for your staff? What creative ideas could you use when training your staff? What could you do to help your staff be self-directed learners?
Strategies for coaching and mentoring staff	*Developing People in Early Childhood Organizations*	Subsection "Principles and Strategies for Coaching and Mentoring" from chapter 2 ("Training Staff")	What strategies do you currently use to coach and mentor your staff? What challenges do you face in coaching and mentoring your staff? How could you empower your staff through strengths-based coaching?
Effectively evaluating staff	*Developing People in Early Childhood Organizations*	Chapter 3: "Appraising Staff"	What strategies do you use to monitor, measure, and evaluate staff performance? Identify the components for giving staff effective feedback.
Fostering teamwork and collaboration with staff	*Developing People in Early Childhood Organizations*	Subsection "Indicators of Effective Teamwork" in chapter 4 ("Promoting Teamwork")	What strategies could you use to foster teamwork and collaboration with your staff? What are the indicators of effective teamwork? What could you do to build trust and respect among your staff members?
Addressing staff-member challenges (turnover, gossip, conflicts, and burnout)	*Developing People in Early Childhood Organizations*	Subsection "Dealing with Staff Conflicts" in chapter 4 ("Promoting Teamwork")	What types of staff-member challenges do you encounter? How do you currently address them? What new strategies could you use to address staff-member challenges? What could inhibit staff from doing their jobs effectively? What did you do to show respect and appreciation for your staff this past month?

YEAR 2

Topic	Reading Assignment	Guiding Questions
Courageous leadership	Note: All reading assignments are from *Leading with Heart and Soul* by Toni Christie. Chapter 1: "Be Courageous" Chapter 2: "Dream Big"	What strategies could you use to communicate with courage and deliver effective feedback? How can our perceptions affect how we deal with conflict? What positive strategies could you use to handle conflict productively? What are your big dreams? How could you make them come true?
Servant leadership	Chapter 3: "Serve Others" Chapter 4: "Have Empathy"	How can you serve others within your organization? What action will you take this week to demonstrate a generosity of spirit? What types of changes are your organization and staff facing right now? How could you use this knowledge to display empathy for the members of your team?
Authentic leadership	Chapter 5: "Foster Loyalty" Chapter 6: "Be Honest"	How could you foster loyalty within your organization? How could you be an honest and authentic leader?
Strengths-based leadership	Chapter 7: "Display Grace" Chapter 8: "Encourage Creativity"	How will you create equality within your team and ensure that all voices are heard? What tasks could you delegate to the strengths of other team members?
Joyful leadership	Chapter 9: "Create Joy" Chapter 10: "Show Gratitude"	How will you create a joyful environment within your program and demonstrate a playful manner? Identify three ways that you will show gratitude to your staff this week.
Respectful leadership	Chapter 11: "Empower Others" Chapter 12: "Model Respect"	How will you empower others to bring about improvements within your organization? How will you model and demonstrate respect for your team members?

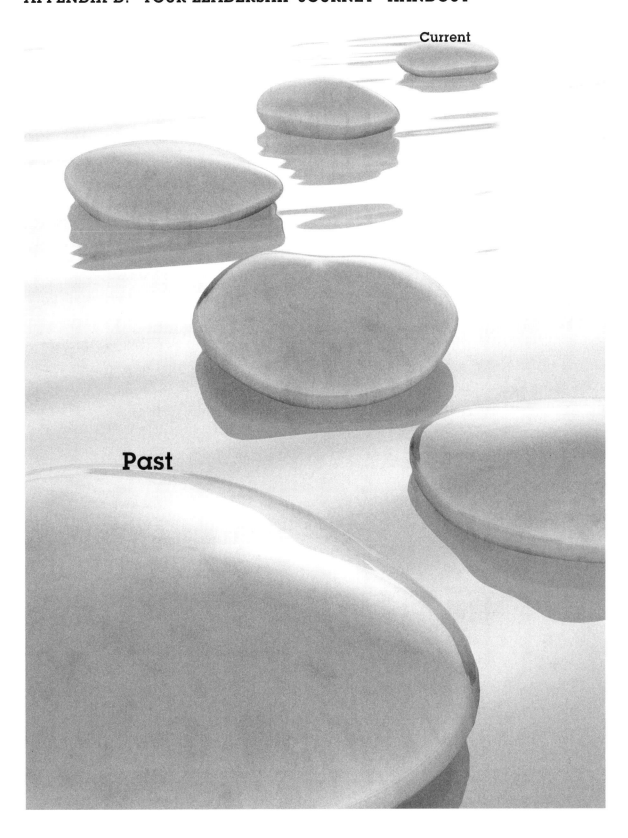

APPENDIX E: RECOMMENDED LEADERSHIP BOOKS

Bloom, Paula, Ann Hentschel, and Jill Bella. 2016. *A Great Place to Work: Creating a Healthy Organizational Climate.* 2nd ed. Lake Forest, IL: New Horizons.

    Examines ten dimensions of organizational climate (such as decision making, collegiality, innovation, supervisor support, and opportunities for professional growth) in early childhood programs.

Bloom, Paula. 2014. *Leadership in Action: How Effective Directors Get Things Done.* 2nd ed. Lake Forest, IL: New Horizons.

    Explores leadership styles, how to strengthen leadership capacity, and how to develop leadership skills and competencies in yourself and others in early childhood programs.

Bloom, Paula, Ann Hentschel, and Jill Bella. 2013. *Inspiring Peak Performance: Competence, Commitment, and Collaboration.* Lake Forest, IL: New Horizons.

    Focuses on five strategies (teacher induction, individual learning plans, peer learning teams, 360-degree feedback, and developmental supervision) that early childhood directors can use to inspire peak performance.

Bruno, Holly. 2012. *What You Need to Lead an Early Childhood Program: Emotional Intelligence in Practice.* Washington, DC: National Association for the Education of Young Children.

    Provides a guide for early childhood program directors on ways to build respectful relationships with families and staff. Covers topics such as financial management, marketing, and connecting emotional intelligence to effective leadership.

Christie, Toni. 2016. *Leading with Heart and Soul.* Wellington, NZ: Childspace Early Childhood Institute.

    Features twelve key values (such as being courageous, serving others, fostering loyalty, displaying grace, showing gratitude, creating joy, and empowering others) for early childhood leadership.

Dweck, Carol. 2006. *Mindset: The New Psychology of Success.* New York, NY: Ballantine Books.

    Explores two different types of mindsets: fixed and growth.

Exchange Press. 2016. *Art of Leadership: Developing People in Early Childhood Organizations.* Redmond, WA: Exchange.

    Compilation of articles on selecting, training, and appraising staff and promoting teamwork. Practical advice from leaders in early childhood.

Exchange Press. 2016. *Art of Leadership: Leading Early Childhood Organizations.* Redmond, WA: Exchange.

    Compilation of articles on topics related to being a leader, supervising staff, and managing early childhood organizations. Practical advice from leaders in early childhood.

Gordon, Jon. 2007. *The Energy Bus: 10 Rules to Fuel Your Life, Work, and Team with Positive Energy*. Hoboken, NJ: Wiley and Sons.

Includes ten ways to approach life and work with positive energy. An engaging story that shows how to overcome adversity and bring out the best in yourself and others.

Jablon, Judy, Amy Dombro, and Shaun Johnsen. 2016.*Coaching with Powerful Interactions: A Guide for Partnering with Early Childhood Teachers*. Washington, DC: National Association for the Education of Young Children.

Outlines coaching strategies that promote positive changes in teachers' practices. Describes the three steps of Powerful Interactions. Includes access to thirty coaching videos.

Loflin, Jones, and Todd Musig. 2005. *Juggling Elephants: An Easier Way to Get Your Most Important Things Done—Now!* New York, NY: Portfolio.

Learn ways to balance your work, family, and personal life just as a ringmaster manages a three-ring circus. Tips on how to focus your time and energy on the most important aspects of your life.

MacDonald, Susan. 2016. *Inspiring Early Childhood Leadership: Eight Strategies to Ignite Passion and Transform Program Quality*. Lewisville, NC: Gryphon House.

Features eight strategies for transforming early childhood programs. Learn ways to motivate and inspire teachers, give nonjudgmental feedback, and become a more confident leader.

O'Neill, Cassandra, and Monica Brinkerhoff. 2018. *Five Elements of Collective Leadership for Early Childhood Professionals*. Saint Paul, MN: Redleaf.

Explore components of collective leadership, including shared decision-making, transparency, and involving the people affected by a change in the change process.

Pink, Daniel. 2011. *Drive: The Surprising Truth about What Motivates Us*. New York, NY: Riverhead Books.

Learn about the three elements of intrinsic motivation: autonomy, mastery, and purpose. Intrinsic motivation can lead to improved productivity and fulfillment.

Sinek, Simon. 2009. *Start with Why: How Great Leaders Inspire Everyone to Take Action*. New York, NY: Portfolio/Penguin.

Examines how great leaders inspire others by putting the *why* (purpose) before the *how* (process) or the *what* (product).

APPENDIX F: COACH-TEACHER PARTNERSHIP AGREEMENT

This is an example of a coach-teacher partnership agreement that has been used in connection with several coaching initiatives. It can be adapted to meet the specific needs of your coaches and teachers.

RESPONSIBILITIES OF COACHES

- Partner with the teacher to implement strong teacher-child interactions.
- Engage in focused observations.
- Reflect with the teacher on current practices.
- Focus on the teacher's strengths, emerging skills, and professional goals.
- Offer strategies for enhancing teacher-child interactions.
- Provide training, materials, and resources.
- Be nonjudgmental and supportive in all coaching interactions.

RESPONSIBILITIES OF TEACHERS

- Partner with the coach to implement strong teacher-child interactions.
- Reflect with the coach on current practices.
- Implement strategies to enhance teacher-child interactions.
- Create and achieve professional goals related to teacher-child interactions.
- Be open to coaching and willing to try new strategies.
- Complete all training, and utilize materials and resources.
- Be nonjudgmental and supportive in all coaching interactions.

Signatures

Teacher _____

Coach _____

Gryphon House
www.gryphonhouse.com

Lose the Lecture: Engaging Approaches to Early Childhood Professional Learning

APPENDIX G: RSBC CONVERSATION PLANNING SHEET

Date: _____   Teacher's Name: _____

C1: CREATE CARING CONNECTIONS (3–5 MINUTES)

Greet: Start with a genuine, enthusiastic greeting that includes calling the teacher by name.

Thank: Thank the teacher for allowing you to observe his/her classroom and being willing to meet with you.

Connect: Ask a connecting question related to the teacher's life.

_____

_____

_____

Outline: Give a brief overview that outlines the flow of the coaching conversation.

Talk (Teacher): Ask the teacher to reflect on the observation and share what he/she thought went well.

Affirm: Affirm the teacher's feedback, paraphrase his/her response, and give positive "I noticed" statements based on the observation.

_____

_____

_____

C2: COMMUNICATE SHARED GOALS (5–7 MINUTES)

Follow Up: Discuss with the teacher the shared goal, plan of action, and reflection from the previous coaching session.

Learning: Ask the teacher questions that link the children's learning and engagement to the shared goal.

Expand: Ask the teacher to share ideas on how to continue to expand children's learning and engagement. Share additional ideas for his/her consideration.

_____

_____

Introduce: Introduce and define the new area of focus.

Reflect (Teacher): Have the teacher reflect on and share how his/her current teaching practices relate to the new focus area (and review assessment data, if available).

New Goal: Discuss with the teacher opportunities for growth, and cooperatively determine a new shared goal, including a desired outcome and a strategy to achieve it.

_____

_____

_____

_____

C3: CONSTRUCT AND EXPAND (15–20 MINUTES)

Plan: Have the teacher start writing down ideas for a plan of action that details how the two of you will work toward the shared goal.

Define What: Check the teacher's understanding of the shared goal by having him/her define the desired outcome and the strategy.

Explain Why: Have the teacher explain why the desired outcome is important for young children's growth and development.

Identify When, Where, and with Whom: Have the teacher flesh out the strategy by identifying when, where, and with whom he/she will teach the skill from the desired outcome.

_____

_____

_____

_____

_____

Model How: Demonstrate the strategy, and expand the teacher's learning by giving other examples of the strategy.

Practice Now: Give the teacher an opportunity to practice the strategy. Check for understanding, clarify, and give feedback.

Reflect (Teacher): Ask the teacher to reflect on how implementing the strategy will make a difference in children's lives.

Set Check-In Date: With the teacher, determine a specific date by which he/she will complete and report on the plan of action and its outcomes.

_____

_____

_____

C4: CLOSING CONNECTIONS (2–3 MINUTES)

Thank: Thank the teacher for his/her time, attention, and efforts.

Encourage: Express excitement and encouragement about the agreed-upon next steps.

Reflect (Teacher): Encourage the teacher to continue to reflect on his/her teaching practices and to plan on sharing his/her reflections at the next coaching session.

_____

_____

_____

Questions: Ask the teacher if he/she has any questions or concerns. If so, address them.

Focus: Make a closing connection with the teacher, and share the focus of the next coaching observation.

Next: Inform the teacher of the date and time of the next coaching session, according to the schedule you have set up with the program administrators.

_____

_____

_____

APPENDIX H: PLAN OF ACTION GEOMETRIC FORM

Name: _____

Date: _____ Focus Area: _____

Shared Goal: _____

Fill out each shape (see next page) as follows:

- **Circle:** *What:* Define the desired outcome (which usually involves helping children build a specific skill) and the strategy (what you will do achieve the desired outcome) from your shared goal.

- **Heart:** *Why:* Explain why the desired outcome is important for young children's growth and development.

- **Hexagon:** *When, Where, and with Whom:* List when and where you will teach the skill from the desired outcome and the specific children with whom you will do it.

- **Diamond:** *How:* List the specific steps you will take and the materials you will need to teach the skill.

- **Rectangle:** *I Noticed . . . :* Write what you notice as you implement this plan of action.

What?

Why?

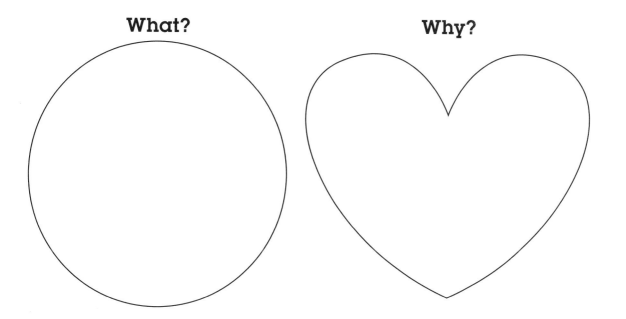

When, Where, and with Whom?

How?

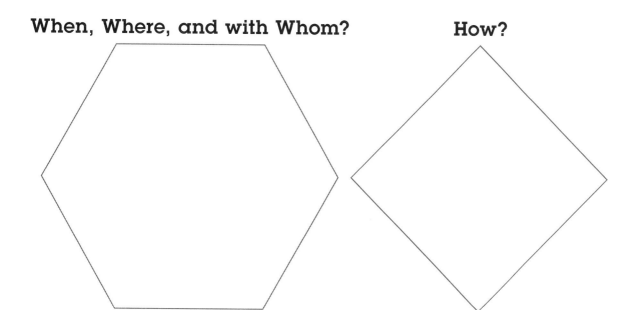

I noticed ...

APPENDIX I: RSBC CONVERSATION REFLECTION TOOL

Item	Yes	No	Notes
C1: Create Caring Connections			
Greet: Did I/the coach start with a genuine, enthusiastic greeting that included calling the teacher by name?			
Thank: Did I/the coach thank the teacher for allowing me/the coach to observe the teacher's classroom and for meeting with me/the coach?			
Connect: Did I/the coach ask a connecting question related to the teacher's life (for example, "How are you doing today?")?			
Outline: Did I/the coach give a brief overview and outline the flow of the coaching conversation?			
Talk (Teacher): Did I/the coach ask the teacher to reflect on the observation and then share what he/she thought went well?			
Affirm: Did I/the coach affirm the teacher's feedback, paraphrase his/her response, and give positive "I noticed" statements based on the observation?			

Gryphon House
www.gryphonhouse.com

Lose the Lecture: Engaging Approaches to Early Childhood Professional Learning

Item	Yes	No	Notes
C2: Communicate Shared Goals			
Follow Up: Did I/the coach discuss with the teacher the shared goal, plan of action, and reflection from the previous coaching session?			
Learning: Did I/the coach ask the teacher questions that linked the children's learning and engagement to the shared goal (for example, "What did you notice about the children's engagement when you did X?")?			
Expand: Did I/the coach ask the teacher to share ideas for continuing to expand the children's learning and engagement? Did I/the coach share additional ideas for the teacher's consideration?			
Introduce: Did I/the coach introduce and define the new focus area?			
Reflect (Teacher): Did I/the coach have the teacher reflect on and share how his/her current practices relate to the new focus area (and review assessment data, if available)?			
New Goal: Did I/the coach discuss with the teacher opportunities for growth and then cooperatively determine a new shared goal, including a desired outcome and a strategy to achieve it?			

Item	Yes	No	Notes
C3: Construct and Expand			
Plan: Did I/the coach have the teacher start writing down ideas for a plan of action that details how we/they will work toward the shared goal?			
Define What: Did I/the coach check the teacher's understanding of the shared goal by having him/her define the desired outcome and the strategy?			
Explain Why: Did I/the coach have the teacher explain why the desired outcome is important for young children's growth and development?			
Identify When, Where, and with Whom: Did I/the coach have the teacher flesh out the strategy by identifying when, where, and with whom he/she will teach the skill from the desired outcome?			
Model How: Did I/the coach demonstrate the strategy (for example, in person, through a video, or with the children) and expand the teacher's learning by giving other examples of the strategy?			
Practice Now: Did I/the coach give the teacher an opportunity to practice the strategy?			
Reflect (Teacher): Did I/the coach ask the teacher to reflect on how implementing the strategy will make a difference in children's lives?			
Set Check-In Date: Did I/the coach, in collaboration with the teacher, determine a specific date by which the teacher will complete and report on the plan of action and its outcomes?			

Gryphon House
www.gryphonhouse.com

Lose the Lecture: Engaging Approaches to Early Childhood Professional Learning

Item	Yes	No	Notes
C4: Closing Connections			
Thank: Did I/the coach thank the teacher for his/her time, attention, and efforts?			
Encourage: Did I/the coach express excitement and encouragement about the agreed-upon next steps?			
Reflect (Teacher): Did I/the coach encourage the teacher to continue to reflect on his/her teaching practices and to plan on sharing those reflections at the next coaching session?			
Questions: Did I/the coach ask the teacher if he/she had any questions or concerns? If he/she did, did I/the coach address them?			
Focus: Did I/the coach make a closing connection with the teacher and share the focus of the next coaching observation?			
Next: Did I/the coach inform the teacher of the date and time of the next coaching session, according to the schedule set up with the program administrators?			

Glows (Strengths)	Grows (Opportunities for Growth)

Lose the Lecture: Engaging Approaches to Early Childhood Professional Learning

APPENDIX J: RSBC CONVERSATION KEY WORD CHART

C1: Create Caring Connections

Greet	Outline
Thank	Talk (Teacher)
Connect	Affirm

C2: Communicate Shared Goals

Follow Up	Introduce
Learning	Reflect (Teacher)
Expand	New Goal

C3: Construct and Expand Learning

Plan	Model How
Define What	Practice Now
Explain Why	Reflect (Teacher)
Identify When, Where, and with Whom	Set Check-In Date

C4: Closing Connections

Thank	Questions
Encourage	Focus
Reflect (Teacher)	Next

APPENDIX K: SAMPLE TRAINING-SESSION OUTLINE

Title of Training Session: "The Social-Emotional Development of Infants and Toddlers"

Session Description: This training session will explore the social-emotional development of infants and toddlers. Participants will learn strategies for helping young children interact positively and manage strong emotions. The session will examine different types of fears that young children experience, such as fear of separation, fear of losing love, fear of body damage, and fear of the unknown.

LEARNING OBJECTIVES

1. Participants will devise strategies to promote children's social-emotional competence.

2. Participants will determine effective ways to support children when they experience fears.

3. Participants will identify calming activities.

MATERIALS

- 1 copy of the "My Social-Emotional Portrait" handout per participant (see appendix P)

- sticky notes

- pens or pencils

- "The Hug That Helped Change Medicine" video:
  https://www.youtube.com/watch?v=0YwT_Gx49os

- "Helping Toddlers Regulate Emotions" video by the Yale Center for Emotional Intelligence:
  https://www.youtube.com/watch?v=-H14NNUYwVc

- 1 set of pictures of children displaying various emotions per small group

- 4 sheets of flip-chart paper titled "Fear of Separation," "Fear of Losing Love," "Fear of Body Damage," and "Fear of the Unknown" (posted on the walls)

- markers

- 1 sheet of unlined paper per participant

- 1 sheet of lined paper per small group

- "Exit Ticket" handout

OUTLINE

Objective	Topic	Engagement Strategy	Time
1	Training-session overview Warm-up connector: My Social-Emotional Portrait Define objectives Outline agenda	My Social-Emotional Portrait: Participants complete their own social-emotional portraits and share them in pairs.	10 minutes
1	Early experiences and social skills	Partner share: What are young children learning from you about social skills?	10 minutes
1	Becoming children's social-emotional coaches	Each participant writes on a sticky note two ways in which she can be a child's social emotional-coach. She stands up, finds a partner, and shares.	10 minutes
1	Emotional connections "Rescuing Hug"	Video: "The Hug That Helped Change Medicine" (https://www.youtube.com/watch?v=0YwT_Gx49os) Large-group discussion on the power of positive physical touch	10 minutes
1	Children's emotions and nonverbal cues	Children's Emotion Pictures: Participants look at pictures of children and think about the emotions those children express. Participants talk at their tables about the nonverbal cues that children communicate.	10 minutes

Objective	Topic	Engagement Strategy	Time
1	Emotional competence	Video: "Helping Toddlers Regulate Emotions" by the Yale Center for Emotional Intelligence (https://www.youtube.com/watch?v=-H14NNUYwVc). Discuss key points from video in pairs.	10 minutes
2	Common fears in young children: • Fear of separation • Fear of losing love • Fear of body damage • Fear of the unknown	Password Triangle: Partners give clues and guess key words related to different types of fears. Round Robin: Participants go to posted charts and write down how they can be children's social-emotional coaches for each type of fear.	10 minutes
1	Strategies for promoting social-emotional competence	Participants create word clouds using synonyms for the emotion words *mad* and *sad*.	20 minutes
3	Calming activities	Small groups each create a top-ten list of ways to help young children calm down.	10 minutes
1	Reflection and Review	Review key points. Participants reflect on training content and complete exit tickets highlighting one thing they learned during the session and one thing they will do to enhance their teaching this week.	10 minutes
		Total session time	2 hours

APPENDIX L: TRAINER REFLECTION TOOL

Rate yourself or the trainer you are observing. For each practice, indicate the level at which you or the trainer implemented the practice (high, mid, or low).

Practice	High	Mid	Low	Notes/Comments
Create a Climate of Caring Connections				
Did I/the trainer welcome learners to the training session using a positive, enthusiastic greeting?				
Did I/the trainer make connections with the learners?				
Did I/the trainer use a warm-up activity to build relationships with learners?				
Did I/the trainer use a positive, enthusiastic tone of voice throughout the training session?				
Did I/the trainer suspend judgment on responses from learners?				
Did I/the trainer effectively respond to learners' comments and questions?				

Practice	High	Mid	Low	Notes/Comments
Present a Prepared and Effective Presentation				
Was I/the trainer well prepared?				
Did I/the trainer state the objectives of the training session?				
Did I/the trainer demonstrate strong understanding of the content?				
Did I/the trainer use a variety of strategies to engage learners?				
Did I/the trainer use various learning techniques that promote retention of information?				
Did I/the trainer give the participants multiple opportunities to discuss content with other learners?				
Did I/the trainer summarize main points?				
Did I/the trainer move around the room during the training session?				
Did I/the trainer reference current scholarly resources during the training session?				
Did I/the trainer provide learners with breaks and brain breaks at least once every hour?				
Did I/the trainer have learners reflect on current practices?				
Did I/the trainer have learners reflect on opportunities that they could take and strategies that they could implement in their classrooms?				

Gryphon House
www.gryphonhouse.com

Lose the Lecture: Engaging Approaches to Early Childhood Professional Learning

Practice	High	Mid	Low	Notes/Comments
Implement Adult Learning Principles				
Did I/the trainer help learners understand the relevance and applicability of the content to their current situations?				
Did I/the trainer allow learners to be self-directed and proactive in the learning process?				
Did I/the trainer provide opportunities for learners to utilize their knowledge and life experiences during learning?				
Did I/the trainer include learning experiences that promoted immediacy of application?				
Did I/the trainer use a problem-centered approach to learning?				

Glows (Strengths)	Grows (Opportunities for Growth)

APPENDIX M: "CLOCK PARTNERS" HANDOUT

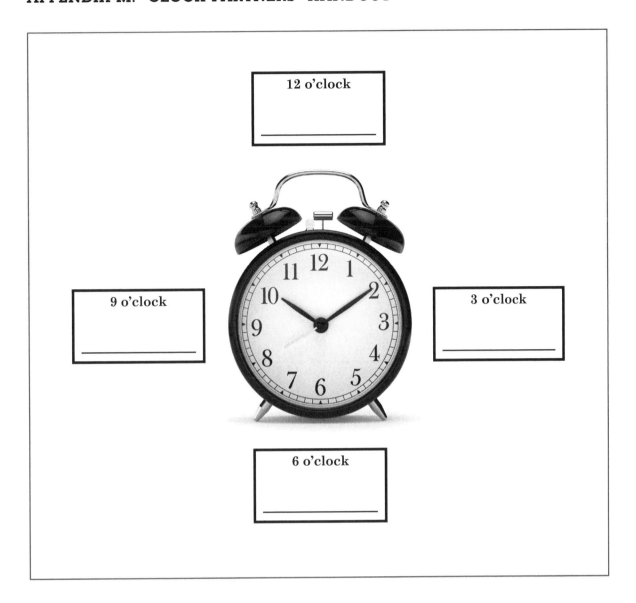

12 o'clock
_____

9 o'clock
_____

3 o'clock
_____

6 o'clock
_____

Clock Partners

Using the clock, make "appointments" with four different people:

- 1 person for the 3 o'clock slot
- 1 person for the 6 o'clock slot
- 1 person for the 9 o'clock slot
- 1 person for the 12 o'clock slot

Write each person's name by the corresponding time.

APPENDIX N: "3, 2, 1" HANDOUT

Write 3 ideas from the reading that you want to share.

1. _____

2. _____

3. _____

Write 2 ideas from the reading that you can apply at your program.

1. _____

2. _____

Write 1 question about the reading that you want to discuss.

_____

Write 3 ideas from the reading that you want to share.

1. _____

2. _____

3. _____

Write 2 ideas from the reading that you can apply at your program.

1. _____

2. _____

Write 1 question about the reading that you want to discuss.

_____

GryphonHouse
www.gryphonhouse.com
Lose the Lecture: Engaging Approaches to Early Childhood Professional Learning

APPENDIX O: VIDEO RESOURCE LIST

These websites have videos related to early childhood education that you could use for training and coaching.

Organization	Description	URL
California Early Childhood Educator Competencies	Thirteen videos to assist child-care providers in understanding and caring for children Available in English and Spanish	https://www.cde.ca.gov/sp/cd/re/ececomps.asp
High Scope	The HighScopePreschool channel features more than thirty videos that highlight teaching practices in preschool classrooms.	https://www.youtube.com/user/HighScopePreschool/videos Find more videos by searching "High Scope videos" on YouTube.
Center for Early Education and Eastern Connecticut State University	More than one hundred videos related to child development Videos available in English and Spanish	http://www.easternct.edu/cece/alphabetical-list-of-videos/
Illinois Early Learning Project	Videos on benchmarks, parenting, guidelines for child-care providers, and infant and toddler learning Available in English and Spanish	https://illinoisearlylearning.org/videos/
Head Start	Videos from Head Start	https://eclkc.ohs.acf.hhs.gov/search/eclkc?q=video

Organization	Description	URL
Centers for Disease Control and Prevention	PSAs about developmental milestones	https://www.cdc.gov/ncbddd/actearly/multimedia/video.html https://www.cdc.gov/parents/essentials/videos/index.html
Center on the Developing Child at Harvard University	Videos produced by the Center on the Developing Child at Harvard University	https://developingchild.harvard.edu/resourcecategory/multimedia/
Teachstone	More than fifty videos produced by Teachstone	https://www.youtube.com/user/InteractionsMatter/videos
Child Care and Early Education Research Connections	Early childhood multimedia resources	https://www.researchconnections.org/childcare/search/resources# (on left side, select "Resource Type" button and click on "Multimedia")
Zero to Three	Early childhood videos	https://www.zerotothree.org/resources (on right side, select "By format" and click on "Videos")
Results Matter Video Library (Colorado Department of Education)	Extensive library of video clips for practicing observation and assessment Some clips available in Spanish	http://www.cde.state.co.us/resultsmatter/rmvideoseries
The Early Childhood Education and Training Program	More than three hundred instructional, informational, and observational videos for early childhood educators and program administrators	https://www.ecetp.pdp.albany.edu/VideoLibrary/VideoLibraryList.aspx
Early Educator Central	Clips for infant and toddler teachers	https://earlyeducatorcentral.acf.hhs.gov/video-clips

APPENDIX P: "MY SOCIAL-EMOTIONAL PORTRAIT" HANDOUT

Enjoyable
Social Activity

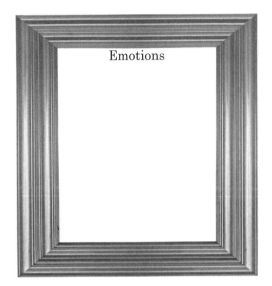

Emotions

Describe Your Happy Place

BFF
(Best Friend Forever)

FEAR

EXIT TICKET

Name: _____

Share 1 thing you learned during the training session.

_____

Share 1 thing you will do to enhance your teaching this week.

_____

EXIT TICKET

Name: _____

Share 1 thing you learned during the training session.

_____

Share 1 thing you will do to enhance your teaching this week.

_____

EXIT TICKET

Name: _____

Share 1 thing you learned during the training session.

_____

Share 1 thing you will do to enhance your teaching this week.

_____

EXIT TICKET

Name: _____

Share 1 thing you learned during the training session.

_____

Share 1 thing you will do to enhance your teaching this week.

_____

REFERENCES

ADA.gov. 2009."Americans with Disabilities Act of 1990, as Amended." ADA.gov. https://www.ada.gov/pubs/adastatute08.htm

Anderson, Lorin, and David Krathwohl, eds. 2001. *A Taxonomy for Learning, Teaching, and Assessing: A Revision of Bloom's Taxonomy of Educational Objectives.* New York, NY: Longman.

Bank Street College of Education Center on Culture, Race, and Equity. n.d. "Our Approach." Bank Street College of Education Center on Culture, Race, and Equity. https://www.bankstreet.edu/our-work-with-schools-and-communities/bank-street-education-center/center-on-culture-race-equity/approach/

Bank Street College of Education Center on Culture, Race, and Equity. n.d. "Professional Development." Bank Street College of Education Center on Culture, Race, and Equity. https://www.bankstreet.edu/our-work-with-schools-and-communities/bank-street-education-center/center-on-culture-race-equity/pd-opportunities/

Blankenship, Selena, and Wendy Ruona. February 28–March 4, 2007. "Professional Learning Communities and Communities of Practice: A Comparison of Models, Literature Review." Paper presented at the Academy of Human Resource Development International Research Conference in the Americas, Indianapolis, IN. https://files.eric.ed.gov/fulltext/ED504776.pdf

Blitz, Cynthia, and Rebecca Schulman. 2016. *Measurement Instruments for Assessing the Performance of Professional Learning Communities (REL 2016–144).* Washington, DC: US Department of Education, Institute of Education Sciences, National Center for Education Evaluation and Regional Assistance, Regional Educational Laboratory Mid-Atlantic. http://ies.ed.gov/ncee/edlabs

Bloom, Paula, Ann Hentschel, and Jill Bella. 2013.*Inspiring Peak Performance: Competence, Commitment, and Collaboration.* Lake Forest, IL: New Horizons.

Bradway, Sarah. 2009. "Vision of an Adult Learner Today." YouTube. https://www.youtube.com/watch?v=tu24QNtRado

Cotton, Gayle. 2013. "Gestures to Avoid in Cross-Cultural Business: In Other Words, 'Keep Your Fingers to Yourself!'" *Huffington Post*, June 13, https://www.huffingtonpost.com/gayle-cotton/cross-cultural-gestures_b_3437653.html

Desimone, Laura. 2009. "Improving Impact Studies of Teachers' Professional Development: Toward Better Conceptualizations and Measures." *Educational Researcher* 38(3): 181–199.

Desimone, Laura, and Katie Pak. 2017. "Instructional Coaching as High-Quality Professional Development." *Theory into Practice* 56(1): 3–12.

DuFour, Richard. 2017. "Building a Professional Learning Community." AASA: The School Superintendents Association. http://aasa.org/SchoolAdministratorArticle.aspx?id=9190

DuFour, Richard, and Robert Eaker. 1998. *Professional Learning Communities at Work: Best Practices for Enhancing Student Achievement.* Bloomington, IN: National Education Service.

Dunst, Carl. 2015. "Improving the Design and Implementation of In-Service Professional Development in Early Childhood Intervention." *Infants and Young Children* 28(3): 210–219.

Dweck, Carol. 2007. *Mindset: The New Psychology of Success.* New York, NY: Ballantine Books.

Dyer, Frank, and Thomas Martin. 1929. *Edison: His Life and Inventions,* vol. 2. New York,NY: Harper and Brothers. https://books.google.com/books?id=B7A4AAAAMAAJ&printsec=frontcover#v=onepage&q&f=false

Easton, Lois Brown. 2016. "Strategic Accountability Is Key to Making PLCs Effective." Phi Delta Kappan. https://www.kappanonline.org/easton-strategy-plcs-professional-development-effective-accountability/

Exchange Press. 2016a. *Art of Leadership: Developing People in Early Childhood Organizations.* Redmond, WA: Exchange.

Exchange Press. 2016b. *Art of Leadership: Leading Early Childhood Organizations.* Redmond, WA: Exchange.

Hemmeter, Mary Louise, Lise Fox, and Patricia Snyder. 2018. *Teaching Pyramid Observation Tool (TPOT) for Preschool Classrooms Manual*, Research Edition. Baltimore, MD: Paul H. Brookes Publishing Company.

Holmes, Oliver Wendell, Sr. 1873. *The Autocrat of the Breakfast-Table.* Boston, MA: James R. Osgood. http://www.gutenberg.org/files/751/751-h/751-h.htm

Jablon, Judy, Amy Dombro, and Shaun Johnsen. 2016. *Coaching with Powerful Interactions: A Guide for Partnership with Early Childhood Teachers.* Washington, DC: National Association for the Education of Young Children.

Jessie, Lillie. 2007. "The Elements of a Professional Learning Community." *Leadership Compass* 5(2): n.p. https://www.naesp.org/sites/default/files/resources/2/Leadership_Compass/2007/LC2007v5n2a4.pdf

Knowles, Malcolm, Elwood Holton III, and Richard Swanson. 2014. *The Adult Learner: The Definitive Classic in Adult Education and Human Resource Development.* London, UK: Routledge.

Lancaster, Lynne, and David Stillman. 2002. *When Generations Collide: Who They Are. Why They Clash. How to Solve the Generational Puzzle at Work.* New York, NY: Harper Business.

Latson, Jennifer. 2014. "How Edison Invented the Light Bulb—And Lots of Myths About Himself." *Time*, October 21, http://time.com/3517011/thomas-edison/

Marino, Vivian. 2006. "College-Town Real Estate: The Next Big Niche?" *The New York Times*, August 20, https://www.nytimes.com/2006/08/20/realestate/commercial/20sqft.html?fta=y

Markussen-Brown, Justin, et al. 2017. "The Effects of Language- and Literacy-Focused Professional Development on Early Educators and Children: A Best-Evidence Meta-Analysis." *Early Childhood Research Quarterly* 38: 97–115.

Maslow, Abraham. 1943. "A Theory of Human Motivation." *Psychological Review* 50(4): 370–396.

Michelini, Michael. 2018. "The Differences between East and West in Terms of Culture and Education." Global from Asia. https://www.globalfromasia.com/east-west-differences/

National Association for the Education of Young Children. n.d. "About Us." National Association for the Education of Young Children. https://www.naeyc.org/about-us

National Association for the Education of Young Children. n.d. "Our Mission and Strategic Direction." National Association for the Education of Young Children. https://www.naeyc.org/about-us/people/mission-and-strategic-direction

National Association for the Education of Young Children. n.d. "Play and Policy Interest Forums." National Association for the Education of Young Children. https://www.naeyc.org/play-and-policy-interest-forums

National Association for the Education of Young Children. 2004. "Code of Ethical Conduct: Supplement for Early Childhood Adult Educators." National Association for the Education of Young Children. https://www.naeyc.org/sites/default/files/globally-shared/downloads/PDFs/resources/position-statements/ethics04_09202013update.pdf

O'Neill, Cassandra, and Monica Brinkerhoff. 2018. *Five Elements of Collective Leadership for Early Childhood Professionals*. Saint Paul, MN: Redleaf.

Opfer, V. Darleen, and David Pedder. "Conceptualizing Teacher Professional Learning." *Review of Educational Research* 81(3): 376–407.

Pink, Daniel, 2011. *Drive: The Surprising Truth about What Motivates Us*. New York, NY: Riverhead Books.

Pollard, Kelvin, and Paola Scommegna. 2014. "Just How Many Baby Boomers Are There?" Population Reference Bureau. https://www.prb.org/justhowmanybabyboomersarethere/

Rockquemore, Kerry Ann. 2010. "There Is No Guru." Inside Higher Ed. https://www.insidehighered.com/advice/2010/04/19/there-no-guru

Rolfe, Gary, Dawn Freshwater, and Melanie Jasper. 2001.*Critical Reflection for Nursing and the Helping Professions: A User's Guide*. Basingstoke, UK: Palgrave.

Schon, Donald. 1983. *The Reflective Practitioner: How Professionals Think in Action*. New York, NY: Basic Books.

Serrat, Olivier. 2008. "Building Communities of Practice." Asian Development Bank. https://www.adb.org/sites/default/files/publication/27564/building-communities-practice.pdf

Sinek, Simon. 2009. *Start with Why: How Great Leaders Inspire Everyone to Take Action.* New York, NY: Portfolio/Penguin.

Sinek, Simon. 2009. "How Great Leaders Inspire Action." TED video. https://www.ted.com/talks/simon_sinek_how_great_leaders_inspire_action?language=en

Smith, Craig. 2018. "145 Important Millennials Statistics and Facts (May 2018)." DMR. https://expandedramblings.com/index.php/millennial-statistics-for-marketers/

Stover, Katie, et al. 2011. "Differentiated Coaching: Fostering Reflection with Teacher." *Reading Teacher* 64(7): 498–509.

Taylor, Paul, and Scott Keeter, eds. 2010. *Millennials: A Portrait of Generation Next. Confident. Connected. Open to Change.* Washington, DC: Pew Research Center. http://assets.pewresearch.org/wp-content/uploads/sites/3/2010/10/millennials-confident-connected-open-to-change.pdf

Wenger, Etienne. 1998. *Communities of Practice: Learning, Meaning, and Identity.* Cambridge, UK: Cambridge University Press.

Wenger, Etienne, Richard McDermott, and William Snyder. 2002. *Cultivating Communities of Practice: A Guide to Managing Knowledge.* Boston, MA: Harvard Business School Press.

Wenger-Trayner, Etienne, and Beverly Wegner-Trayner. 2015. "Introduction to Communities of Practice: A Brief Overview of the Concept and Its Uses." Wenger-Trayner.com. http://wenger-trayner.com/introduction-to-communities-of-practice/

Western Governors University. 2014. "Professional Development vs. Professional Learning: How to Become a Better Teacher." *The Night Owl Blog* (blog). Western Governors University. https://www.wgu.edu/blogpost/professional-development-vs-professional-learning-teachers

Wheatley, Margaret. 2002. *Turning to One Another: Simple Conversations to Restore Hope in the Future.* Oakland, CA: Berrett-Koehler Publishers.

Williams, Lucy. 2017. "How to Accept and Respect Other Cultures." Owlcation. https://owlcation.com/social-sciences/How-to-Accept-and-Respect-other-Cultures

World Bank. n.d. "Communities of Practice Questions and Answers." World Bank. http://siteresources.worldbank.org/WBI/Resources/CoP_QA.pdf

Zorn, Eric. 1997. "Without Failure, Jordan Would Be False Idol." *Chicago Tribune*, May 19, http://www.chicagotribune.com/news/ct-xpm-1997-05-19-9705190096-story.html]

INDEX